DAILY
MEDITATIONS

Front cover: pixelsteve for Pixabay.com

Prosveta S.A – 83600 Fréjus (France)
ISBN 978-2-8184-0515-4
original edition: 978-2-8184-0514-7
digital edition : 978-2-8181-0562-8

Omraam Mikhaël Aïvanhov

D A I L Y
MEDITATIONS

2021

P R O S V E T A

Foreword

Every morning, before you do anything else, you must give yourself a few quiet moments of reflection so as to begin your day in peace and harmony, and unite yourself to the Creator by dedicating the new day to Him through prayer, meditation.

It is the beginning that is all-important, for it is then, at the beginning, that new forces are set in motion and given direction. If we want to act wisely and well, we have to begin by casting some light on the situation. You do not look for something or start work in the dark; you start by lighting a lamp so that you can see what you are doing. And you can apply the same principle to every area in life: in order to know what to do and how to do it, you have to switch on the light – in other words, to concentrate and look into yourself. Without this light you will wander in all directions and knock on many different doors, and you will never achieve anything worthwhile.

Our days follow the direction that we give to our first thoughts in the morning, for, depending on whether we are mindful or not, we either clear the way ahead or litter it with all kinds of useless and even dangerous debris. Disciples of initiatic science know how to begin the day so that it may be fruitful and rich in God's grace, and so that they may share that grace with those around them. They understand how important it is to begin the day with one fundamental thought around which all the other thoughts of the day may revolve.

If you keep your sights fixed on a definite goal, a clear orientation, an ideal, all your activities will gradually organize themselves and fall into line in such a way as to contribute to the realization of that ideal. Even the negative or alien thoughts or feelings that attempt to infiltrate you will be deflected and put at the service of the divine world. Yes, even they will be forced to follow the direction you have chosen. In this way, thanks to the fundamental thought that you place in your head and your heart first thing in the morning, your whole day will be recorded in the book of life.

And, since everything we do is recorded, once you have lived one glorious day, one day of eternal life, not only will that day be recorded, not only will it never die, but it will endeavor to get the days that follow to imitate it. Try to live just one day as well as you possibly can, therefore, and it will influence all your days: it will persuade them to listen to its testimony and follow its example, so as to be well balanced, orderly, and harmonious.

Omraam Mikhaël Aïvanhov

Between 1938 and 1985, Omraam Mikhaël Aïvanhov elaborated a spiritual teaching in almost five thousand improvised talks. His words have been preserved in their entirety, as the talks given between 1938 and the early 1960s were taken down in shorthand, and the later ones were recorded on tape and latterly on video.

Many of these recordings have been published in book form by Prosveta, providing a comprehensive guide to the teaching.

GLOSSARY

Definitions of terms as used by the Master Omraam Mikhaël Aïvanhov:

Brotherhood: a collectivity governed by a truly cohesive spirit, in which each individual works consciously for the good of all. (Daily Meditations 2007: 24 February) A brotherhood is a collectivity whose members share the common bond of a broad, luminous consciousness and work with and for each other, and more than that, they work for the whole world. True brotherhood is universal.

Caduceus: the two snakes represent the two currents, positive and negative, of astral light known traditionally as Od and Ob. The one is luminous and hot, the other is dark and cold; one is white, the other black. (Izvor 237 ch. 9)

Collectivity [human]: a group of people, usually quite extensive, united by a common interest, a common organization or common sentiments, or living in the same place or country. (Prosveta, France, provided it)

Collectivity [cosmic]: the totality of beings in the universe, both visible and invisible.

Disinterestedness: refers not to a lack of interest but to an altruism, an absence of bias motivated by interest or advantage. This is a central part of the Master's philosophy. (A New Dawn, part 2, p.120)

Entities: disincarnate beings, drawn to humans and to nature. They may be either light or dark beings, depending on the quality of the vibrations of the person or place attracting them.

Higher Self, Lower Self: must be understood within the context of the Master's teaching concerning the two natures in human beings, the human lower self and the divine higher self, which he calls respectively personality and individuality. (Love and Sexuality, part 2, p. 42)

Impersonal: refers not to a coldness of attitude but to the absence of referral to self.

Individuality: see 'higher self, lower self'.

Personality: see 'higher self, lower self'.

Psychic: (adjective – as in 'psychic life / world / bodies, etc.'): refers not to mediumship but to a human being's subtle energy beyond the physical, i.e. heart and mind (and soul, or soul and spirit, according to the context).

The Rock: a platform at the top of a hill near the Bonfin, where the Master and his disciples gathered every morning, in spring and summer, to meditate and watch the sun rise.

1 January

Last night, as you left your friends, you wished them good night, saying, 'I'll see you next year!' And now, only a few hours later, it is next year. You already speak of yesterday as 'last year'. All day yesterday, until the very last second before midnight, in fact, until eleven fifty-nine and fifty-nine seconds, it was still the old year. On the stroke of midnight, the New Year began.

If you take the time to think about this, you will make some interesting discoveries. A single second divides one year from the next. However, before you reach that final second, you have to go through the long succession of days that lead up to it. Well, you should know that the transformation of a human being follows the same pattern. Yes, the spiritual transformation of a human being happens in the blink of an eye. In no more than a split second, a person can be totally renewed and regenerated, but this crowning moment can come only after they have worked and striven towards it for hundreds and thousands of years.

Just as with the year gone by, the period leading up to the moment of transfiguration will be referred to as the old life; and just as with the New Year, the period dawning at that moment will be known as the new life. How long will we have to wait before this final second arrives? You need not worry about that, it will come for each one of you. So be patient, you must learn to wait. But while waiting you must work.

2 January

*A*ll human beings without exception seek consciously or unconsciously to give meaning to their lives. We all need a reason for existing, and we try to find it every day in all the different aspects presented to us by our family, social and professional lives.

But in reality, neither material success nor possessions can give them the meaning of life for in fact it is a 'sense', and sense is not something material. We can find it only very high up on the subtle planes. Lower down, we can only find forms. Of course, the feelings and sensations born of a great love for an object, a person or an activity can give content to a form, but feelings are volatile, and sooner or later, we are left to suffer from a sense of emptiness. So we must look beyond the content for the meaning. Once you have found meaning, you have found fulfilment.

3 January

A truly spiritual person will never give up the divine work they have begun whatever may come to pass. Even amid the worst ordeals, they say to themselves, 'Here is yet another opportunity to mobilize all these hostile forces and harness them to my own work.' Yet, through sheer carelessness, most human beings manage to demolish all the positive gains they have made even when nothing bad befalls them. They create and destroy, create and destroy, over and over, which is why they never achieve anything.

To obtain results, you must persevere in your spiritual work. That is to say, you have to put everything to use – the good and the bad, the joys and sorrows, hope and discouragement. Yes, everything must be at the service of this work. This can truly be called building, because each day brings new elements.

4 January

When disciples sincerely embrace the spiritual life, it doesn't matter to them whether or not people know about their work; they are not interested in playing a role or letting others know what they are doing. The only thing that counts for them is their work, but not in the human world, in the world of light. Many people, who do not put work first, want immediate recognition for their efforts. They want to be useful in order to earn praise.

So their motives are rather personal. Of course, it is difficult to overcome the desire to be appreciated completely. Yet, it is precisely when disciples are no longer interested in glory and are fully immersed in this marvellous work without thinking of anything else, that they begin to win the appreciation of heaven and are allowed to take part in the councils on high. Those who reach this point can wish for nothing greater.

5 January

Disciples know that as they are on earth for a very short time, it is not worth wasting their energy seeking honours, titles and possessions that they will only have to abandon when they leave. Instead, they try to concentrate on everlasting, indestructible riches, which they continue to accrue until their departure from the physical plane. As a result, they accumulate such great wealth in their subtle bodies that they go straight to the regions of light where they acquired the particles for these bodies.

For there is a law that says if you draw within you a great deal of heavenly material, one day, you will have to go to the region from which it came. Due to the law of affinity, these very materials will usher you into the subtle regions where you will spend an eternity of joy discovering the splendours of the universe.

6 January

The goal of an initiatic school is to point human beings back in the direction of their Father's house, towards that 'secret place of the Most High' mentioned in Psalm 91: 'My refuge and my fortress, my God, in whom I trust', for that is where they will be safe, where the forces of evil can no longer reach them.

But it seems people do everything to distance themselves from this high shelter where they are under God's protection. They are eager to live their own lives, turning away from the Lord and breaking his laws. Well, this proves that they still have a great deal of suffering to endure, which is why they do not want to enter into the divine light to be protected. Yes, if they have this tendency always to be out of step and to disobey, it is simply because it is decreed by their fate that they must suffer. Whereas those who have already suffered a lot and learned their lesson do everything they can to return to their Father's side in this most high dwelling place – or in a spiritual brotherhood or an initiatic school, which is in fact the symbolic return to a divine order.

7 January

Inner strength, balance, peace and happiness all depend on love. But you must sense that love is there within your reach, that it is inside you, and that there is no reason to ever feel poor and lonely. If you do feel poor and lonely, then you have not learned to detach yourself from the physical plane. As soon as you enter onto the subtle planes, especially the regions of the soul and the spirit, it is impossible to feel lonely, for the universal Soul and the universal Spirit are always there, in and around you, and you can communicate with them at any time. Whereas can you ever be sure that a man or a woman – even the best – will not have to turn their attention to other matters and be forced to leave you at some point?

So, even if you have found the most wonderful person on earth, don't leave it at that. Thank heaven for allowing you to meet such a being, but know that you will experience true love only once you manage to find it in the regions of the soul and the spirit.

8 January

You must improve yourself in order to improve the quality of your seeds. 'What seeds?' you will ask. Your thoughts and feelings. Each one of your thoughts, each one of your feelings is a seed that reflects your strengths and weaknesses, and you sow these seeds all around you wherever you go.

The ground on which all these seeds fall is found on the astral and mental planes, and one day when you visit these regions, and ask, 'Where have all those thistles and thorns come from?' you will be told that they are your crop, that you are the one who planted them. 'And these roses and lilacs and lilies?' Well, it will also be explained to you that they too are your work: the good thoughts and feelings you scattered around you.

9 January

When you dial a telephone number, only one of millions and millions of people answers – the person with this number. The relationships between all beings in the universe obey this law. Just as a person answers when you dial their number, so does a specific entity communicate with you because you have emitted a thought that vibrates in unison with it; a connection is established between you and the being or place on which your thought is focused.

All those whose thoughts are always chaotic and conflicting are bound to have unfortunate encounters because they come into contact with entities that correspond to these thoughts. This is why it is very important to fill your mind with a heavenly idea, for that idea will magically attract all the beings and elements capable of contributing to its realization. A sublime idea in one's mind is like a warning sign to the spirits of darkness – 'Beware of the dog', 'Occupied', 'Keep out' – and they dare not enter; but it leaves the door wide open to all the spirits of light.

10 January

Jesus said, *'You are the temples of the living God'*, but human beings are accustomed to worshipping in inanimate temples of wood or stone, and they do not tend to their own temple – themselves, their entire being.

Of course, thanks to the fervour of all the faithful who have come to pray in these temples throughout the centuries, there is still some life in them. But they cannot compare to a human being who has managed to strengthen their will, purify their heart, enlighten their intellect, expand their soul and sanctify their spirit, for such a being has become a true temple. It is when you are a temple, when you pray in your own temple that God listens to you and answers your prayers. And if at the same time, you are conscious of being in this other temple, the universe, then you will become a whole being, you will have achieved fulfilment.

11 January

You must rid yourself of this awful habit of taking, always taking. Make an effort to think about giving. Try at least to look at others with love, to give them a smile and to draw a few beneficial particles from your heart to cast their way. By doing so, it is you yourself who will feel rich and happy.

Human beings are always afraid of losing something, of becoming poor; they do not understand that it is in fact this miserly attitude that impoverishes them. To become rich you must give. Yes, by taking we impoverish ourselves, and by giving we become richer because we activate unknown forces that are lying dormant and stagnant somewhere deep within us. In our desire to share them with others, they begin to stir, to flow, and we then feel so enriched that we are astonished. We think, 'How can this be? I gave and I gave, and I am richer for it!' Indeed, for this is the new life.

12 January

*I*t is in prayer, in the act of praying, that you must find happiness, knowing that the day your prayers are answered, you will no longer have the happiness of asking. When our wishes come true, there is nothing more to rejoice in, and we miss those wonderful days of the past when we waited for something marvellous, picturing it in our imagination. This is why you must find all your happiness in the bond your prayer creates between you and heaven, otherwise, God only knows if you will be happy once you have obtained what you asked for.

People who understand the true meaning of prayer will always be happy, even if they have nothing, because no one can stop them from creating extraordinary things in the subtle world of thought, things that will always stay with them because they remain out of reach.

13 January

Love possesses extraordinary power for those who are able to understand it and manifest it. Love alone knows everything, fixes everything, triggers and projects unimaginable forces.

It is said that God is Love. But when we see the human tragedies born of love, we realize just how much work still needs to be done, how much distance we still need to travel in order to raise ourselves up to this divine love. But it is worth it, for love is the true and almighty magus. You must invite love to come and dwell within you, and then, like the flame that shines through the glass of a lamp, it will shine and spring forth all around you wherever you go.

14 January

The closer we get to the centre, to the spiritual sun, the more we feel light, warmth and life growing within us. This is a law. And it means that if you feel darkness, cold and death descend on you, you need not look far for the reason – it is because you have drifted away from the centre.

Initiatic Science teaches us that true strength lies in knowing how to remain at the centre. In humans, this centre is the highest point, the summit of our being. The periphery on the other hand is where we encounter unrest and distress when our consciousness strays towards things that are alien to our true self – to our soul and spirit. This is why we must keep a constant watch over ourselves and say, 'Let me see, where am I today? Oh, I have wandered off towards the periphery. What awaits me there?' Nothing good, that is for sure, which is why you must hurry back to the centre. How? Through prayer, through meditation, by consciously establishing a bond with the sublime Centre, with God himself.

15 January

Concentrating on light is one of the most effective, most powerful exercises there is. But never forget that the effect something has on you depends on your attitude towards it. If you consider it useful and magical, you amplify its effect. Through your thoughts and convictions, you have a decisive influence, which is indeed far more important than the objects or conditions themselves.

Light can penetrate you without your being aware of it of course, but if you are attentive and full of good-will to participate in its work, with the conviction that something is growing and developing within you, you will gradually sense the vibration of new forces.

16 January

*T*hose who work tirelessly to beautify, enrich and harmonize their inner being feel at ease within themselves. They may even welcome guests to this splendid dwelling. Yes, luminous spirits are delighted to pay them a visit!

Look how receptions are organized in everyday life. If you receive your guests in pleasant surroundings, offering them delicious meals, strolls through the gardens and concerts, won't they look forward to coming again? Well, it is the same with the spirits of light. If they find a dwelling within you where beauty, harmony and purity reign, they will come to visit you. They may even settle there permanently, and it is you who will benefit from their presence.

17 January

*T*he only reality for human beings is what they feel and experience. Take the case of someone who has hallucinations: they scream in terror because they feel that they are being chased by monsters. Visibly, no one is physically attacking them, but they feel persecuted and are suffering, and when someone is suffering, try telling them that it is all an illusion!

Then there are those who experience ecstasy and illumination in spite of appalling conditions. There again, how can you convince them that they are deluding themselves? The sufferings and joys people experience are perhaps the only things they never doubt. We can doubt what we see, what we hear and what we touch, but we can never doubt the reality of what we feel and experience.

18 January

It is true that we live in a society in which a great many things need to be changed, but this must not be achieved through violence. Besides, true change is never wrought through violence, which always leads to greater evils than those it claims to cure.

So, how can we bring about change in society? By our way of life. It is by first transforming themselves that human beings can change the whole world. But for this to happen, they need a Teaching, that is to say, a system and methods. For this is the crux of the matter: you have to live a new life based on a new philosophy supported and nourished by a new understanding of love. Harmony then begins to take root in people who become beneficial, constructive agents for all of humanity.

19 January

A spiritual Master, an Initiate, bears enormous responsibilities but he is not crushed by them, for spiritual responsibilities are not heavy or burdensome. If you want to spread light in the world, it may seem as though you are burdening yourself, but in reality, things become lighter for you. Why? Because the nature of the charge is different. Far from weighing you down, responsibilities of a divine, spiritual nature lift you up. It all depends on the nature of the charges you accept.

Take for example a block of stone; it is heavy because it is subject to the gravitational force of the earth, but if you move it far enough from the earth to escape this attraction, it becomes weightless – it is light enough to float. So, if you know how to transport your burdens beyond the reach of the earth's gravity, not only will they cease to weigh you down, but they will lift you up like a balloon, higher and higher. When a Master asks you to free yourself, he means that you must free yourself from all your prosaic, mundane activities in order to take on divine charges that will lift you up.

20 January

*I*n order to assert their freedom, human beings want to break down all the moral barriers erected by the initiates of the past, which were designed to protect them against the disorder of their passions. But people are so ignorant that they do not realize that this kind of disorder consumes their divine energies. For in order to feed the fire that possesses them, they are obliged to give it all they have got, all their resources and materials. It is a furnace that is fed by the very substance of their being. They cannot throw their neighbour's goods or the trees of the forest into this fire; it can burn only their own reserves, their own fuel, their own quintessence. In order to sustain these states of effervescence and these volcanic eruptions day in, day out, they are obliged to burn their most precious energies. They do not know that they lose something of their intelligence, purity, strength and beauty each time. In the end, when everything is spent, they find that they have become stupid, ugly, weak and sick.

The initiates did not give human beings these rules and methods to rob them of their freedom, but to save them from falling into such a state of wretchedness.

21 January

Learn to bless beings and objects. Think to impart only beneficial influences to everything you touch, to everything you do. Instead of taking selfish pleasure in caressing the head of someone you love, transform this gesture into spiritual work by saying, 'May God bless you. May light reign in this head; may the angels come and dwell here.' In this way, the sensual, voluptuous element of your love will be transformed into an extraordinary feeling such as you have never known. And when you touch your child's head or its little arms and legs, why not bless them so that angels come and make of them a magnificent being?

You must bless everything you touch: objects, food and living beings. This is true white magic.

22 January

*E*ach human being can be compared to a drop of water, and each drop of water falls exactly where Cosmic Intelligence intended it to fall so as to accomplish its task.

Each drop has to sacrifice itself in one way or another, by quenching the thirsty, refreshing those who are hot, washing those who are dirty after a day's work, watering the seeds in the fields, and so on. Yes, the sacrifices demanded of water are many – it is used to make bread, cook food and even to dissolve poison – and it must never rebel against what is asked of it; it must always accept. When it has fulfilled its mission, it can return to the heavens and become transparent again. The same is true of human beings.

23 January

*H*uman beings are not in the habit of spending their time in activities that could change their lives. They neglect meditation, contemplation and prayer even though these practices could improve their lives by releasing forces within them capable of transforming and neutralizing their negative states.

Yet, even with regard to our physical health, it is much better to live the spiritual life. Take away a person's spiritual life and all that is left is the biological life that enables them to eat, sleep, and move about. Without that intense inner vibration to stimulate and vivify them, even their physical functions gradually begin to slow down and become sluggish, thus producing a build-up of waste that overloads their organism. So, if only for the sake of your health, try to live an active spiritual life.

24 January

*E*very human being imagines, dreams and wishes. When the imagination comes into play, a series of images passes through one's mind, each one called up by association with the one before it. And since everyone imagines, everyone thinks they know what the imagination is. But they are mistaken. True imagination, such as the initiates conceive it and with which they work, is a kind of screen located at the boundary between the visible and invisible worlds, and on this screen are reflected objects and entities that normally escape our consciousness. Certain highly evolved human beings, who know how to direct this faculty, express many of the things received and recorded by their imagination. Much later on, we realize that what they had thus 'imagined' was not pure invention on their part – they had captured realities that had yet to appear on the physical plane.

If human beings learn to work on their own thoughts and feelings, they can purify their mental body to such a degree that their imagination becomes crystal-clear – pure and transparent – and they begin to 'see'. At this level, imagination and vision are one.

25 January

*E*verything exists within a single cell. As in a seed, all that will one day appear and take shape is already there contained as potential. Our organs and our five senses all developed in this way, and still more will appear in the future. Given that the physical body is created in the image of the other subtler bodies, and that we have five senses on the physical plane, this means that we also have five senses both on the astral plane and on the mental plane.*

So, once human beings become fully developed, their ability to see, feel, hear, taste, act and move will be astounding. And that is what life is about. A living being, a living cell, or even a simple microorganism contains infinite possibilities, but it takes thousands of years for this potential to blossom. This is the mystery, the splendour of life.

* See plate and note on p. 396 and 397.

26 January

*T*he whole of a person's destiny is determined by their attitude towards heaven. But, far from glorifying God and humbling themselves before his greatness, human beings show less and less respect, thereby obstructing his designs and disrupting the order of creation. Humans' worst enemy is pride, this insolent, arrogant attitude that will lead to their ruin.

If they wish to save themselves, they must learn to regard creation as sacred, to vibrate like an Aeolian harp in response to every breath, every current from heaven, to communicate with the universe, with the Universal Soul, with God himself. During this exchange with the higher world, energies work on their being and infuse their soul with elements of the utmost purity. All traces of darkness are absorbed, lost in Immensity.

27 January

*A*ll those who have truly embraced the philosophy of the Initiates have manifested themselves as well-balanced, peaceful and luminous beings, so why would we not turn back to this philosophy now?

You will say, 'But this is the philosophy we already live by!' You may well believe this, but if you analyze yourselves, you will see that you are still captivated by all sorts of concerns that are far from spiritual. You appease your consciences by accepting a few bits of the Initiates' teachings, but you mix them up with all kinds of trivialities, with whatever a certain politician, intellectual or artist said, wrote or did. I am not saying that you should take absolutely no interest in such matters, but there are things of much greater importance! Yes, it is far more important to take an interest in the creatures that inhabit the luminous regions of space, in their work, and in the laws that govern the future of humanity. For the essence of life is there – not in what the newspapers, radio or television say, but in the essential, eternal world, in which we are one day destined to participate.

28 January

*A*n unknown, insignificant member of society has no power to intervene in affairs of state. In order to be able to do so, you have to reach the centre (or the top, which is symbolically the same), where the king or the president is, and become their minister. Once you have reached the centre, the summit, then, yes, you will have every possibility, but as long as you remain on the fringes, nobody will listen to you.

The same law exists on the spiritual plane. Until you manage to reach the centre – your spirit – you can acquire a few things, to be sure, but you are not really in charge. Whereas if you attain the centre, your spirit, you are the master because this centre affords you every power, everything depends on you. So, stop focusing on transitory, futile realizations and set to work to reach the centre, without worrying about how long it will take you to get there.

29 January

The Church comforts the poor, the weak and the sick by telling them that if they have faith in God, they will be seated at his right side in Paradise. Picture it: the Lord in his heaven surrounded by poor, miserable wretches in rags.

Unfortunately for Christians, the Lord chooses to be surrounded by splendour, by only the most luminous, most powerful and purest creatures. So, instead of relying on being seated at the Lord's right hand, you would be well advised to set to work to activate the spiritual powers within you, for it is they that will enable you to obtain what you desire. When you plant a seed, all the powers of heaven and earth combine to bring forth the flowers and fruits you hoped for. But however strong your faith, if you fail to sow any seed, nothing will grow.

30 January

*T*he intellect is a faculty that allows us to know the physical world and a little of the psychic world, but no more, and as such, it is very limited. The intellect alone cannot know the truth. To know the truth of a rose is not just a question of perceiving its shape, colour, and scent. The truth of a rose is its soul, its emanation, its existence, which the intellect cannot grasp. To know a rose, we must penetrate all the elements that make it a rose.

The same is true of a human being; the truth about someone encompasses everything about them – their soul and spirit, their thoughts and feelings, their plans for the future and so on. As long as you do not know all these things, you do not know the truth about a person. You know a little bit about them, their appearance, but not the truth. The truth is a synthesis, which can only be grasped by the spirit.

31 January

Sometimes, a very lofty, very spiritual desire can trigger an immediate reaction of opposition from your lower nature. The higher and lower worlds are closely linked, and a magnificent aspiration on high can awaken opposing forces and desires in the roots of your being. Of course, if disciples are knowledgeable and enlightened, these schemes of their lower nature have less chance of being successful, for they know that while they are working, meditating and building, they must surround themselves with beings who keep watch over them and protect them. A highly evolved disciple takes the necessary precautions.

Moreover, in the early forms of Freemasonry, which were based on true science, the mason at work was portrayed with a trowel in one hand, and a sword with which to defend himself in the other. So, while the mason worked, he kept watch to ensure that no enemy slipped in and captured the fortress under the cover of darkness.

1 February

*M*any people unwittingly carry out the plans of people they do not even know. You will say that you cannot see how this is possible, but it is very simple. Thoughts and feelings are active forces that can influence those whose psychic structure can pick up the waves that others send out. This explains how many weak people end up committing crimes; they are driven to it by the power of the negative thoughts and feelings others have projected. And since human justice is not clairvoyant, it does not punish those who cast these criminal thoughts and feelings into space; it punishes those who carry them out, even though they are not the real culprits. Of course, they are guilty of having let themselves go and becoming so weak that they can be used as instruments of evil currents, but other people are the true instigators of these crimes.

So, pay attention to your thoughts and feelings, for they could well be put into effect by others, and if they are bad, it is you who will be held responsible by divine justice.

2 February

*I*n winter, when the life of a tree retreats into its roots, the tree becomes dull and bare, without beauty or fragrance, and nobody comes near it. But as soon as the sap begins to rise, birds sing in its branches, and people pause to admire it and sit beside it. This is a lesson that we would all do well to meditate on. When you see people sinking more and more into their roots, that is to say giving priority to their lusts, passions and pleasures, it means that they are already marching towards a spiritual winter. And when others begin to avoid them, it is because they have gradually lost their beauty, inner light and vitality. Unfortunately, they themselves are often the last to understand why.

So, bear this well in mind: as long as you let your energies fuel prosaic, selfish concerns, you will inevitably stagnate, because you will sink into winter – a cold, dark winter in which all movement comes to a halt.

3 February

There is no science more exalted than the science of the divine Word, which treats the twenty-two elements, the twenty-two forces represented by the twenty-two letters of the Hebrew alphabet. The Cabbalah tells us that it is with these that God created the world.

To learn the science of the divine Word is to learn how to combine its twenty-two elements in the three worlds in such a way that they create harmony in our thoughts, feelings and actions. When there is disorder within us, it is because the 'words' are jumbled up or poorly combined. Very few human beings possess the science of the Word, that is, the science of the correspondences between the letters and the forces. Those who possess this science and who know how to arrange these letters are able to establish a true bond between heaven and earth.

4 February

On the pretext that they love their children, some parents do not want to let them suffer or burn themselves a little in order to learn a lesson. At the slightest little thing, they rush to their rescue and shield their children from the consequences of their actions. Well, this is not love. The Lord does not behave in this way, and neither does nature.

The love of parents for their children does not mean immediately sparing them every difficulty. When children get themselves into scrapes, they should be left to struggle for a while and try to work it out. Once they begin to understand why and how they got themselves into the predicament, and to regret what they did, then you can come to the rescue. The fact that they have suffered a little will make them decide to be more careful and sensible in the future. Not only do parents who fail to behave this way do their children a disservice, they actually encourage them to be weak and wicked.

5 February

*F*eelings rather than thoughts drive human beings to act, because by nature, feelings always want to express themselves through actions. Take one of the most common examples in everyday life: a man may think of a woman, but as long as he has no feelings for her, he leaves her alone. But then he begins to feel something, and since feelings refuse to wait, off he races to meet this woman, buy her flowers and court her.

It is difficult for thought to influence the physical body without using feelings as an intermediary. If your actions are inspired purely by reason, your motives may be perfectly clear, but your heart will not be in what you do. We can act without our feelings being involved, but we will not have much of an appetite for it, and sometimes, we may even forget why we are doing it. But if our feelings are involved it is a different matter! Of course, this does not necessarily mean that we know better, and we often make things worse by forging ahead blindly, but at least we know what is driving us!

6 February

*P*eople who have learned to use their five senses correctly – sight, hearing, smell, taste and touch – have a good knowledge of reality.

But this knowledge can also be useful to them in their dealings with others, which is undoubtedly the area where most mistakes are generally made. For they can use their eyes to observe the nature of those they meet. Their ears can perceive and analyze the vibrations and intonations of voices, even on the telephone. Their sense of smell can alert them to the kind of people who live in a given place. Their sense of taste enables them to avoid dangerous encounters, and when they shake hands with someone, they are immediately informed of that person's character and temperament, because a handshake expresses the whole being.

7 February

You carry your little problems around with you wherever you go – 'I have a pain here or there; I need this or that' and so on. Why do you always dwell on what you are lacking instead of on what you already have? Why not remind yourself every day that you have arms and legs, a mouth, eyes and ears? Why not tell yourself that you have been given a divine teaching, that you possess heaven and earth; that you are rich and that life is beautiful?

Every day you should remember that you are a child of God and that you have the power to become once again what you were in the distant past, when you first emerged from the bosom of the Eternal. You fell from this original state because, like the prodigal son, you wanted to experience for yourself what life was like far from your father's house. But now you can go back to him. This return to the Father is what is known as the 'reintegration of beings'. It is in this reintegration that humans become almighty again, that they recover their mastery of the forces of nature and their dignity as God's heirs. This is our true destiny. So, why do you always dwell on the little things you are lacking?

8 February

If you work on the idea of loving, doing good, forgiving and creating harmony around you, the day will come when this idea becomes so powerful that it will permeate all your cells, and they will begin to vibrate in unison with it. You will then notice that you are always at peace, and even if disturbing events occur from time to time, they will create only a few ripples on the surface; deep down, you will always have this sense of peace.

Have you ever seen wild animals at the circus? As long as their tamer is there, they behave; but as soon as the tamer leaves, they are ready to pounce on each other. Well, you should know that the same thing happens with your cells. As long as you keep an eye on them, they obey you, but the moment you turn your back or drop your guard, there is trouble. This means that you must take care of your cells – you must subdue them, nourish them and purify them, as though they were your children. Only when you have succeeded in training them to do their work without quarrelling or arguing will you finally experience peace.

9 February

You must learn to manifest love, to project love to the whole world just as the sun does. All suns bombard each other across space with their rays.

Of course, we are a long way from being able to manifest such love. The earth is dark; it does not know how to shine and has not yet learned to use weapons of light. As such, the war on earth is terrible. But the war waged by the sun produces fruit and flowers and all kinds of wealth. We have not yet learned to wage war in this way. This is why we must go every morning to see how the sun uses its weapons, how it launches them, how with its cannons, mortars and rockets, it gives life to the entire universe.

10 February

*T*he Cabbalah tells us that the face of the first man was that of the Creator himself. Later on, when the intellect awakened in man (a process symbolized by the serpent coiled around the Tree of the Knowledge of Good and Evil), he left paradise. He descended into the denser regions of matter where he experienced cold, darkness, sickness and death, and his face changed. So, now that he is no longer the faithful image of God, he has lost his power; the spirits of nature no longer obey him and instead take pleasure in tormenting him.

If man, one day, manages to recapture the face that was his at the beginning, all the spirits of the universe would submit to him once more. Until then, he will continue to resemble the prodigal son in the parable who, having left his father's house to travel the world, ends wretchedly as a swineherd. But at least the prodigal son finally understood that he should return to his father's house. What about you? Will you ever understand that you must return to the source in order to recapture the light, love and life of your heavenly Father?

11 February

Nowadays, human beings are mainly interested in cultivating their intellectual faculties, which is fine. Unfortunately, they do so at the expense of other means of exploration, and as a result, the subtle life of the universe, the soul and the spirit, eludes their investigations. As they descended into matter, they forgot their divine origins; they no longer remember how beautiful, powerful, luminous and noble they once were. They are interested only in the earth – plundering and destroying it to get rich.

But a time is coming when, instead of always focusing their attention on the outer world, they will turn back to the path of inner exploration. They will lose none of the knowledge acquired over the centuries, but they will no longer concentrate exclusively on the outer aspects of the universe. Humanity's descent into matter will remain an extraordinary achievement, but human beings will not stop there. They will go on to discover other deeper and even more essential regions.

12 February

Stop identifying with your physical body. Your physical body is not you – it is nothing more than your vehicle. The reason why so many human beings lose their bearings and fall apart is that they continually identify with what they are not. The body, physical matter, is subject to decay, and if you identify with it, you too will decay. Whereas if you identify with your immortal spirit, you become a spark, a flame, and you can overcome all difficulties.

Human beings do the greatest harm to themselves in their willingness to identify with corruptible, ephemeral matter instead of identifying with the spirit, which is immutable and eternal. When the spirit leaves the physical body, it continues to exist. The physical body is merely the instrument that has been given to the spirit so that we might live on earth.

13 February

*T*houghts are living entities. Some of them die very quickly, while others endure for a very long time, depending on the force with which they were initially formed. Some thoughts can even survive for centuries. There are all kinds of these entities, so be careful, pay attention, and maintain strong ties with the sublime world.

If you leave your mind, your soul or your heart open to all the vagrants in space, they will prey on you. Conversely, if you know how to prepare yourself inwardly, you will attract only beneficial influences that will accompany you and be a constant source of inspiration and joy. Disciples who know these things seek out the company of luminous entities willing to help them in their work.

14 February

*T*he solutions human beings have found to the problems inherent in collective life are purely superficial. Outwardly, they have formed nations and organized societies whose members support each other, and in which each individual contributes to the good of the whole and benefits from it. Yet inwardly, individuals remain isolated, aggressive and hostile towards one another. They have not learned how to transpose the material, practical progress achieved, or their skills in the areas of organization and technology, to their inner lives. That is why, despite all this progress, humanity is still suffering from the same evils – war, poverty, famine and oppression – on a scale unheard of until now.

It is essential to understand once and for all that no real improvement can come about without a profound change of mentality. Only when human beings feel themselves united psychically and spiritually will they succeed in forming a true society: a universal brotherhood within themselves. When each individual strives to attain the higher consciousness of unity, then societies, peoples and nations will begin to live in freedom and happiness.

15 February

*E*ven the great beings of the past are obliged to go to school and learn everything anew when they return to earth. This may surprise you, but it is a law: all beings who incarnate on earth, whoever they may have been in the past, must begin their education and apprenticeship all over again. What sets them apart from others is that they obtain great results very quickly, but everyone, without exception, must take up their work at the beginning again if their qualities are to manifest themselves in this lifetime.

If Mozart had not been born into a family of musicians who could give him the conditions he needed to learn and perfect the gifts he brought with him from the past, his genius would perhaps not have manifested itself so brilliantly. However great the wisdom and powers possessed by initiates in a previous incarnation, they must still work to regain that knowledge and those powers. And if that is true for them, those who have yet to reach such a degree of evolution must work all the harder!

16 February

*C*rystals and precious stones are the quintessence of the earth. Flowers are the quintessence
of water. Birds are the quintessence of air.
Initiates, who represent the Deity on earth, are
the quintessence of fire. And finally, beyond
fire, the quintessence of ether, that is to say, the
quintessence of all these quintessences, is the
angelic host that reaches up to God, this whole
hierarchy of beings that Jacob saw in his vision
going up and down the ladder between earth and
the Throne of God.

The Scriptures say that man must become
a jewel in the crown of God. This is a symbol.
Precious stones are attached to the earth and
are nourished by the earth; flowers cannot live
without water; birds dwell in the air, and human
beings die if they are not in contact with fire. Fire
is the food of the initiates. When Zoroaster asked
the god Ahura-Mazda what primordial man ate,
Ahura-Mazda replied, *'He ate fire and drank
light.'*

17 February

*A*ll the sciences must be placed in the service of the one science truly worth studying: that of the human being. Today, unfortunately, it has been abandoned in favour of physics, chemistry, astronomy, biology, and so on. You will say that the sciences of human anatomy and physiology are at least worth something. Of course, but these basic sciences study the physical framework of human beings, not the human being as a whole.

A change of point of view is necessary. From now on, the whole human being must be considered as the centre of the universe, including the divinity that dwells within him. All the other sciences must contribute to this one science; they should no longer be considered independently because in reality, a human being is a summary of all that exists, and all the sciences converge in him. Once this new point of view is established in the minds of thinkers, all of existence will be transformed. Instead of focusing on the externals, on all that is material, rigid and lifeless, life itself with all its subtle aspects will be given top priority.

18 February

If we lived in the sun, perhaps there would be no shadows. But we have left the sun and come down to earth, and the earth revolves around the sun, thus creating the alternation of light and shade. Since we are outside the sun, we have to accept this alternation: day and night, light and dark, activity and rest, good and evil. Not only must we accept it, but we must also know how to use it.

How do you use the night? Marvellously – you sleep, you do nothing, and in the morning when you wake up, you have regained all your strength, your body has rid itself of its waste and you are once again ready to begin work. So why can't you also learn to use evil, darkness and difficulties? To use evil, you must integrate it, that is, you must incorporate it into your work as raw material, just as a chemist uses all substances, however toxic. Everything can be useful.

19 February

*G*od has given human beings the possibility to
make infinite progress... to become just like him.
Unfortunately, most people have a deplorable attitude that prevents them from using this possibility.
It is as though they were chloroformed. Yet no one
is absolutely bound hand and foot – even the most
limited creatures possess the means to surpass
themselves – and if they would only turn their
eyes and their thoughts to the Lord, they would
discover their own possibilities. Of course, it all
depends on what kind of things you want.

If what matters most to you are material things –
success, money, and pleasure – if there is no room
in your mind for spiritual values, you will never
make any progress. But when someone puts love,
beauty and the spirit before everything else in their
life, without worrying about whether they will be
rich or poor, well dressed or in rags, honoured or
ridiculed, then for them, everything is possible.

20 February

According to an Arabic proverb, there are four categories of human beings. The first category is made up of those who are so mentally limited that they do not know that they do not know. Nothing can be done for such people – leave them be. In the second category are those who know that they do not know; they are sincere and full of good will – teach them. The third category is made up of those who are asleep, they do not know that they know – wake them up. And in the fourth category are those few, very rare beings who know that they know. These are the sages and the initiates, and the proverb says, 'Follow them!'

21 February

*O*bserve yourself and observe others, then you will notice that when people accept a spiritual teaching, however exalted it may be, after a month, six months, or a year, depending on the individuals concerned, they begin to have contradictory reactions. They are ill at ease, irritated, or they rebel. Instead of intensifying the positive aspects of their nature, their spiritual work seems only to accentuate the negative. Why? Because each new thought, each new feeling is liable to ferment in those who have not prepared themselves to receive them.

When Jesus said, *'No one puts new wine into old wineskins; one puts new wine into fresh wineskins'*, he was expressing the same idea: human beings have to prepare new forms within themselves capable of receiving and sustaining a new philosophy, new ideas, a new teaching. In other words, they have to attune themselves to that philosophy in advance, and strengthen and prepare their stomach, lungs and head – their entire physical and psychic organism – so that they can withstand the tension caused by the advent of new currents.

22 February

It is essential for you to know how to achieve the synthesis of form and force: the form has to be protected so as not to be shattered by spiritual forces, and at the same time, the fire of the spirit must be maintained so that it can continue to animate the form. Those who cling to static forms are swimming against the tide of evolution; sooner or later, they will be swept away by the cosmic currents.

All the philosophies and teachings that have become set in their old forms will be carried off by the surging forces of renewal. Everything must be renewed; there is no hiding place on earth for those who refuse to evolve.

23 February

You can only become truly clairvoyant when your heart begins to love, for true clairvoyance, your true eyes, are found in your heart. What do you see in someone you love? Things that nobody else sees. Love opens our eyes. When a woman loves a man, she sees him as a divine being – and do not try to tell her she is wrong! To all appearances that may be true, but if she exaggerates the beautiful qualities of the one she loves, it is because she sees him as he was when God first created him, or how he will be when he returns to the bosom of the Lord.

We have not yet realized to what extent love has the power to open our eyes. If you wish to become clairvoyant, you must learn to love. Like the blind men of the Gospel, your heart must cry for help – 'Have mercy on us, O Lord' and one day when cosmic light answers, 'What do you want me to do for you?' you will say, 'Lord may our eyes be opened!' 'Very well.' And your eyes will be opened.

24 February

The most useful aspect of an initiatic teaching is that it gives us the means to improve our future incarnations. Those who do not understand how useful such a teaching can be will not only fail to improve anything, but they will also be in danger of losing the few advantages they already have.

Take the case of a rich man: if he does nothing good with his wealth, if he is interested only in the pleasures of an ordinary life, he will have to endure great material difficulties in his next in-carnation. He will not even know that he was once very rich and that his present sorry lot is due to the fact that he did not use his wealth to help others. And this law does not only concern financial fortunes; it applies to all forms of wealth – intel-ligence, beauty, physical and psychic health, and so on. A great many people come into the world with terrible handicaps simply because they did not know about this essential truth of initiatic science: that they themselves are the artisans of their own future.

25 February

Very few things are truly necessary in life. We have to wear clothing to protect our bodies, but however much we may like ribbons and lace, they cannot be considered essential. We need the shelter of a house that has walls, a roof and windows; pictures, carpets and knick-knacks may add an aesthetic touch, but they are secondary. And to nourish ourselves, very few kinds of food are really indispensable. If so many different dishes exist, it is because variety is pleasing to the palate. In the Lord's Prayer, Jesus said, *'Give us this day our daily bread'*. He did not ask for butter, cheese or sausages, no, just bread – he mentioned what was essential.

We need very little to sustain life: bread, water, air, light and heat. If we transpose these basic elements onto the spiritual and divine planes, we shall find everything we need for perfect fulfilment. All the rest may be good, but it is not essential.

26 February

Good and evil are harnessed together to keep the wheel of life turning. If only good existed, the wheel would not turn. Yes, good is incapable of doing the job without a helping hand from evil. You might object that evil pulls in the opposite direction to good, but that is just the point – it has to do so!

Consider this simple gesture: when you want to cork or uncork a bottle, you use both hands working in opposite directions. One pulls or pushes at the cork while the other exerts an opposing force on the bottle, and their combined effort enables you to insert or remove the cork. This collaboration between the two opposite forces happens every day before our very eyes, and we must give pause and meditate on it.

27 February

*T*he circle with a point in the centre is a structure that exists throughout the universe. It is that of the solar system, in which the sun is the centre. It is also found in cells, which consist of a nucleus, a substance known as cytoplasm, and a surrounding membrane. It exists in fruit: in the centre there is the seed, then the pulp, the juicy flesh that we eat, and finally the skin or the husk. Every living organism is made up of a centre, surrounded by a space in which life circulates, and finally a 'skin' that serves as a boundary, an outer limit.

From the solar system all the way down to the atom, we find this same structure: the circle with a point in the centre. The space surrounding the point represents matter; without this space, matter could not exist. But the spirit has no need of space; the power of the spirit lies in being an infinitesimal point that is active everywhere at all times.

28 February

*H*uman beings are always worried about the future; they are always wondering about whether they will have the food and shelter they need, whether they will have enough money, and so on. They are so absorbed by all these preoccupations that they neglect far more important matters – they neglect their health, they run roughshod over people and things, they break the laws of love and justice, and they no longer care about anything spiritual. As a result, every day leaves a trail of unresolved problems and mistakes for which no reparation is made. All these things pile up until people are overwhelmed and crushed.

This is why Jesus told us not to worry about tomorrow. If you see to it each day that your conduct is impeccable, the following day will not be cluttered up with unfinished business, and you will be free to do what you want, while taking care not to leave any loose ends behind for the next day. In this way, each new day will find you free and well disposed. You will be ready to work, to study and enjoy yourself, and your whole life will take on a marvellous hue of happiness and blessedness. To put it in a nutshell, by taking care to do everything properly today, you are indirectly taking care of tomorrow.

1 March

*O*ur spirit must travel in order to learn and perfect itself. This is why, from one incarnation to the next, not only is our gender different but we are also born into different countries, different social classes, and different religions.

So, what possible sense is there to the fanaticism of nationalism, class conflict, or holy war for the true faith? None of these notions rests on solid, objective foundations. The spirit travels freely through space. In their blindness, human beings have created artificial barriers between races and cultures, but these narrow points of view will eventually disappear, for their claims are without foundation. Only those who work for unity, for the kingdom of God on earth are on the right track.

2 March

*I*t is said in Initiatic science that anyone who has not been the target of evil's utmost hatred cannot receive the supreme initiation. Yes, you must be hated and opposed by evil and if, despite its attacks, you continue to follow a divine path, this proves your noble elevation.

If evil detests you, it means that you are not its ally; if you were, it would protect and coddle you, rocking you to sleep so as to keep you by its side a little while longer. But if you escape its clutches and refuse to be at its service, then you incur its enmity. Moreover, it is precisely this enmity that can be your stepping-stone to great heights. All the great initiates have encountered the implacable, relentless hatred of evil. But those who knew how to interpret this could see in it a clear sign. Of course, the ignorant pitied them and deplored their destiny, but those who understood rejoiced and said, 'They are destined to reach the heights.'

3 March

Why do you always set your sights on attaining easy successes that do not last? Instead, why not work to achieve something of unimaginable splendour? You are willing to devote five, six, or even ten years to becoming a lawyer, an engineer, a scientist or a doctor, but what is the true value of such an ideal? Besides, what is ten or twenty years? There are goals to be aimed for in life nobler than a university degree – even if a degree confers social standing and material security.

Why not focus your attention on a spiritual quality? You may need centuries to develop it, but it will be a constant beacon to light your path. Divine goodness, patience, purity, integrity, beauty and so on – it will take you more than ten or twenty years to earn diplomas such as these. But this is precisely what you should work hard towards, for that which is difficult, virtually unattainable even, is what will allow you to make continual progress.

4 March

*E*vil will not exist forever. It exists as evil only as long as the Lord gives it the right to; but as soon as He orders it to disappear, it will disappear. Good alone is eternal; evil is transient, but we human beings do not have the power to make it disappear. God alone possesses this power.

God does not need the help of human beings who are too weak and ignorant – the weapons we possess are ineffectual. Since only God can oppose evil, we must let the divine enter us, manifest itself, and work through us. It is the divine within us that will ensure that good takes the place of evil.

5 March

*H*owever great your knowledge, if your life is not in harmony with the laws of nature, this knowledge will slip from your grasp. However, if you possess the science of life that is taught in initiatic schools, your being will be flooded with eternal, universal, cosmic knowledge, and each day will bring new discoveries, new revelations.

This knowledge is already within you, but it is so deeply buried that it can be brought to the surface only if you lead a harmonious and divine life – no need for books or years of study, this life gives you all the essentials. This is why I say that if you rely only on book learning and forget about living in harmony with heaven, all your knowledge will fade and disappear. Even the talents you already possess will be lost. If, on the other hand, you decide to make every effort to live in harmony with the divine world, true knowledge will come and dwell within you.

6 March

You must learn to live with your ideal as though it were already a reality, but at the same time not forget that you are living on earth. It is very important to unite these two aspects in your life – to be completely committed to your divine ideal without losing sight of earthly reality. This is true equilibrium and it is very rarely achieved. Most people are either idealists who cannot see the ground they walk on, or materialists who see nothing else.

The advantage of a spiritual teaching is that it trains people to understand that they are on earth because they have work to do here, whilst their whole being is directed toward the realization of their divine ideal. They become one with this ideal; they merge with it without losing touch with the world. These are the men and women of the future.

7 March

When people are distressed, or have been insulted or offended, they find it normal to be upset and even to cry. But when they experience true beauty, a painting, music, a poem, or a landscape, convention forbids them to show their emotions; they would be ashamed to shed a tear. Well, I say that it should be the other way around – we should be stoic and unmoved in the face of sorrow or offence, but capable of showing emotion and shedding tears in the presence of beauty.

For the tears prompted by beauty are a blessed dew, a shower from heaven, magnificent currents that purify you and water the flowers of your inner garden. Tears of disappointment and bitterness may bring you some relief, but no more than that. Tears of wonder, however, are infused with divine power.

8 March

*T*he main difference between the different realms of nature – minerals, plants, animals and human beings – is their degree of sensitivity, for evolution is directly proportional to sensitivity.

Plants are more sensitive than stones, animals are more sensitive than plants and human beings are more sensitive than animals. But the chain of beings does not end there: above and beyond human beings are the angels, archangels and divinities. There is a whole hierarchy of increasingly sensitive beings all the way up to the Lord himself. The Lord is omniscient; He feels, sees, and knows everything because He alone is truly sensitive. These are the true dimensions of sensitivity. The only being who is truly sensitive is the Lord.

9 March

A temple or a church is simply a form. Religion is the principle, this consciousness of the bond that exists between human beings and God. Those who are fixed on the form feel the need to enter a temple in order to pray and be heard by God. But those who are guided by the principle know there are temples that take other forms: all of nature, with its mountains, oceans and forests, is a temple in which they can pray.

But nature is still not the best temple. There is a temple even superior to nature, and that is you yourself. It is this temple you must purify so that the Lord will come and establish his dwelling there. This is what Jesus meant when he said, *'You are the temple of the living God.'*

10 March

*I*t is important to understand what I mean when I tell you not to come down from the heights. You might say, 'Yes, of course; I always keep myself on a higher plane. I never reach out to others or try to help them. I am very careful to maintain my prestige and dignity.' But that is not at all what I mean. For me, to stay on a higher plane means to be unfailingly noble, fair and generous. The heights I am talking about are your inner nobility and light.

On the physical plane, we are constantly obliged to go up and down, but on the plane of our inner being, we can always avoid going down, that is, giving in to our baser instincts, or doing something illicit or ignoble. You must not be like those haughty, disdainful, uncaring people who never stoop to offer a helping hand. Instead, take an example from the sun; for the sun reaches down to us and sends us warmth and light, it sends us messages of love, it sends us its soul and its very life, but the sun itself remains forever on high.

11 March

We have been told that we should not struggle against evil, and many people do not understand what this means. It means that we must not confront evil on its own turf, for that is where it is strongest, and we would inevitably be defeated. But if we succeed in rising above evil, and raining down fire and lightning from above, it will flee!

Human beings possess an extremely strong inner fortress that is superbly equipped to withstand attacks. This fortress is the realm of light. Who is to prevent you from putting evil to flight by shining a light on it? Why stand there doing nothing? When people let themselves go, the forces of darkness rejoice, saying 'What a wonderful opportunity to feast!' This is how some people allow themselves to be devoured by dark spirits. When this darkness draws near, true disciples defend themselves by projecting light, and this light drives out the darkness.

12 March

*Y*ou can never lose what you truly possess. You can only lose what does not really belong to you, what has not yet fully become a part of you.

It happens that at one moment you believe and at the next you doubt, at one moment you are in the light and a moment later you are in darkness, at one moment you love and then your love vanishes. This means that neither faith nor light nor love belong to you. It is you yourself who have to become faith, light and love. When Jesus said, *'I am the light of the world'*, he identified with light. He did not say that the light was in him or with him – he said that he was the light. Meditate on the important lesson contained in these words.

13 March

You have received such a profusion of truths from this Teaching that you have not even had time to assimilate them all, and yet you are constantly expecting something new. But what are you doing with all that you already have? You must not be content to take notes and file them away somewhere. You must put these truths into practice or you will spend your life waiting for something new, instead of advancing.

The spiritual life requires that we continually work at the same truths. The novelty lies in what we discover each day by delving into them more deeply.

14 March

*T*he physical or psychic constitution of someone who does not behave reasonably is like the wooden framework of a house that is riddled with woodworm: the worms do not destroy it overnight, but years later, the house suddenly collapses. This pattern can be seen in many areas – not only in the lives of human beings but also in entire countries. Often, it is only when we look back centuries later that we can see how a country gradually decayed. Those who lived through the decline were unconcerned because they were blind to what was happening.

Those who base their evaluation of a situation on a short span of time are bound to be mistaken in their judgements because they cannot see how the laws work. One isolated segment of a long process is not a reliable basis for judgement. To understand how the laws work, you have to observe people and events over a long period of time.

15 March

*P*eople who are in love use every means in their power to monopolize and keep the one they love, even to the point of tormenting them and using violence to impose their will on them. But what can anyone actually keep with such methods? How can you prevent others from getting to know your beloved? The opportunities to meet and talk to other people are endless, and if you are not reasonable and understanding, you will suffer. You are like someone who has a park full of flowers – you cannot contain their fragrance or stop people from breathing it in. In fact, what you are guarding so jealously is only the body of your beloved, their envelope, their outer shell.

And the same is true for those you dislike and want to bring down – what can you actually take hold of? The essence of a human being, that is to say, their thoughts and feelings, cannot be shut up and locked away. All around us, we see people making the most ridiculous efforts to grab hold of human souls, but the soul cannot be seized. A physical body can be possessed for a time, but not the mysterious being who dwells within it.

16 March

*F*rom time to time, ask yourself whether you are justified in thinking that you are on the right track. Are your thoughts, feelings and actions above reproach? What proof do you have that you are so wonderful? Is your intellect lucid and unclouded? Is your heart full of love for the Creator and all creatures? Is your will so strong that no one can stop you from attaining your ideal? If you are honest with yourself, you will have to admit that your intellect does not understand much of anything, that your heart is torn by conflicting passions, and that your will is pulled in all directions. So, how can you believe that you are on the right track? There are criteria by which to judge this, but who wants to know about them?

A man may have made a mess of his life; he may be miserable, sick, embittered, without friends or money, but that does not matter – his philosophy of life is faultless! Who says so? He himself, of course. Well, it is not for him to pass judgment but for the circumstances and events of his life to do so. Those who find themselves perpetually in the grip of insoluble problems should conclude that their philosophy is at fault, and that they would do well to change it.

17 March

*B*efore taking care of her child, a mother must first turn her thoughts to God and establish contact with heavenly life. For it is not enough for her to look after her child's physical wellbeing, to nurse it, dress it, wash it, and put it to bed. She must inject a spiritual element into everything she does for it. If she concerns herself only with its ordinary needs, and keeps it away from God, she will turn it into an ordinary child.

A mother who truly wants to nurture and educate her child properly, must go to God and say to him, 'Lord, I come to you so that you might give me light, love, health and celestial beauty for my child.' This way, she will be able to give her child the pure and luminous particles it needs to become a truly exceptional being.

18 March

Learn to live in unison with the harmony of the cosmos, in communion with the soul of the universe, for it is in this universal life that you will find fulfilment.

Some will say that they would rather find fulfilment in love. Yes, but on condition that they do not cut their love off from universal life the way most men and women do, and seek to set themselves apart from everyone, even from heaven. If lovers try to hide, it is because they sense that their behaviour is not very proper. You will say, 'Do you expect them to make a spectacle of themselves in public?' Of course not. What I mean is that human beings should abandon this very narrow and selfish notion of love that leads them to isolate themselves from others and even from all the intelligent forces of heaven that gave them this love. It is a pity that they do not know how to live in harmony with the soul of the universe by giving thanks and glory to heaven, for a love in which the forces of heaven have no part already bears within itself the seeds of its own destruction.

19 March

*T*he older people get, the more lucid, luminous and powerful they can become. If this is not what we typically see, it is because human beings are so used to identifying with their physical body that they submit passively to all its trials and tribulations. However, for a truly spiritual person, it is just the opposite: their thinking becomes increasingly vital and active, for they have learned to free themselves from the constraints of the physical plane and identify with the spirit.

The spirit is all-powerful, the spirit is immortal, the spirit is omniscient, and when you identify with it, matter no longer has the same hold on you. Our physical body must obey the laws of matter, but the spirit is under no such obligation. That is why age is no disadvantage for a spiritual person; on the contrary, their thinking becomes freer and more active on the subtle planes.

20 March

A disciple is someone who, thanks to the visible or invisible presence of their Master, is conscious of being in contact with a higher principle that transforms everything within them.

The life that subsequently emanates from them is the life of the spirit, and as this life springs forth, even their physical appearance begins to change, becoming increasingly harmonious, expressive and luminous.

21 March

Love is a form of energy, the source of which is on high. Love is of the same quintessence as the sun, and our task is to receive this energy and let it flow freely through our being before sending it back to its source in heaven. If this energy does not flow as it should, it is because men and women's inner channels are clogged with the impurities created by their unbridled instincts and passions. Instead of returning to heaven, this energy sinks into the ground and is lost. If, instead of being wasted, this endless stream of energy that descends daily from on high is to complete its circuit and return to the heights, men and women must attain self-mastery, be pure and be truly united with God.

Once you understand how the universe is built, that heaven is both the point of departure and the destination, matter will no longer present an obstacle for you.

22 March

How many of you are really conscious of what it means to be in a spiritual teaching? How many of you understand what we are doing here? You pray, you meditate, you watch the sunrise, you sing in choir and you eat together, but do you know why? It is because all this is part of the programme I have prepared for you. Because I ask you to do these things, you do them to please me. From now on, try to do them for yourselves, with the absolute conviction that you are accomplishing something truly beautiful and sacred that will bear fruit. Remember that the work you are doing here for the light awakens the consciousness of people throughout the world.

Nothing, no single thought or conscious feeling is without effect. The psychic world is like an immense ocean into which pool the thoughts and feelings of all human beings. These thoughts and feelings are living entities, which, depending on their nature, create either beneficial or harmful currents that influence the psyche of all living creatures. Of course, you must not delude yourself and imagine that within a few years you will have changed the world. But our prayers, meditations and singing do produce a light in the invisible world, and this light can help others to find their way out of the darkness.

23 March

Nature closes its doors to those who do not respect it, that is, who seek only to exploit it for their own narrow and selfish ends. Yet this is exactly the attitude human beings have towards the earth, water, air, the sun and the other planets. Do you really think that the conquest of space is driven by altruism?

Many people will say that they do not care if nature closes its doors to them. Perhaps, but if they continue this way, nature will not only close itself off to them, it will strike back. Then, they will have no choice but to understand and change their attitude, which expresses a lack of intelligence, a lack of love, a lack of will – a lack of everything. A lack of intelligence because they fail to understand the laws of nature; a lack of heart because if they loved the beings that inhabit nature, they would not be so cruel as to destroy them; and a lack of will because they always choose the path of least resistance.

24 March

*I*f you realized what a marvel your physical body is, if you knew in what workshops your organs had been built, if you knew how much work the spirit had put into them, and how much it cost the Creator to perfect the whole system, you would take better care of it.

You will say that you are careful, that you eat healthy foods and you exercise, that you get plenty of sleep and so on. Perhaps, but take for example a man who owns a fancy car. He takes great care of it, always choosing the best quality fuel, the best tyres, and so forth – but when he gets behind the wheel, he is neither careful nor in control of himself. He drives recklessly, tearing around at top speed and slamming on the brakes, and before long, his poor, mishandled car breaks down. So, it is not enough to give your body the best food or the best material conditions. If you truly want to be healthy, you must be attentive, farsighted and careful drivers. In other words, you must avoid impassioned states and the negative, discordant thoughts and feelings that are so detrimental to your organism.

25 March

When we look at the various regions of the universe, we find that what differentiates them is the vibrational frequency of their constituent particles. From the mineral kingdom to the human kingdom and beyond, through the angelic orders up to the throne of God, life manifests with ever-increasing intensity and subtlety. This is why we can say that the intensity of a person's life is a measure of their degree of evolution. However, because most human beings do not understand this truth, they live in slow motion. Their lungs, liver, heart and brain – everything about them is stagnant.

To live in slow motion is the most dangerous thing you can do. People who live in slow motion are like a slow-turning wheel – it gets caked with mud. Make your wheel spin faster and it will throw off the mud.

26 March

What ruins most people is their fondness for sordid activities, pleasures or subjects of conversation that drag them down to the lower levels of the astral and mental planes. It is as if something inside them relishes all that is harmful to them, and they carry on even knowing that it will lead to their downfall. You will say that it is impossible to change our predilections. True, it is very difficult, but there is still a method that can help you to do so. Instead of struggling head on against your partiality for things that demean you, try to find ways of kindling a love of light, a love of a high ideal that will uplift and enrich you, and make you more beautiful.

No human being has come to earth loving only heavenly things. Everyone is tempted, particularly in their youth, by dubious pleasures to some degree. This is normal. What is not normal, however, is to stagnate on that level. For an initiate, a person's degree of evolution is measured by their ability to elevate their aspirations, to aim their desires ever further, ever higher.

27 March

*P*lants do not grow in winter, even though the soil is full of seeds, because there is not enough warmth and sunlight. But in the spring, as warmth and light increase, all those seeds begin to grow. You know this, you have seen it, but you still have not understood anything, for if you had, you would have drawn your own conclusions – you would have observed that the same phenomenon occurs within you. For there are seeds in you too, the seeds of the qualities and virtues that God sowed within you from the very beginning, but they do not grow because you do not seek to expose yourself to the rays of the spiritual sun.

This is why we go to watch the sun rising every morning in spring and summer, for the sun is the purest image of the Divine, and in this way, we give the seeds within us the best possible conditions in which to grow and manifest themselves. As for those who believe themselves to be intelligent and learned enough to scorn this practice, their seeds will remain buried for all eternity.

28 March

*T*ry to understand that love is a state of consciousness. This is worth meditating on – for years even – if you want to further your evolution. As long as you do not know love as a state of consciousness, you will remain blindfolded and in darkness, never understanding what life is about.

Of all the qualities that can help bring you closer to this state of consciousness, purity is the most important. Purity means thoughts and feelings that are devoid of selfishness. The three words – life, love and purity – are linked. Why? Because life depends on love, and the purer this love is, the richer, brighter, more beautiful and abundant life is. The meaning of life is to love and be loved. When your love for others is pure, you are like a fountain of life for them, just as those who love you bring you life too.

29 March

God first sent Moses to teach human beings justice. Later, he sent Jesus to teach them love and forgiveness. True, but we must not leave it at that. Turning the other cheek so it may be struck then forgiving is a great improvement over the law of retaliation – 'an eye for an eye, a tooth for a tooth' – but there is still progress to be made.

If someone tries to attack you, there is no law against showing this person that you are stronger than they are. Lift them by the scruff of the neck and ask them, 'Do you want me to smash you to the ground?' Instead of throwing them, put them gently on their feet again – thanks to this display of strength, they will begin to respect you. Would this not be much better than always allowing yourself to be mistreated and defeated? You must be stronger than your enemies, capable of paralyzing them with a single gesture, glance or word and making them feel so small and wretched that they beat a retreat. When you cannot win on the physical plane, you can at least try to win on the mental plane. This is certainly far better than letting yourself be destroyed by dishonest, unjust and cruel people.

30 March

You can live in society, in fact, you must live in society, but you must hold fast to light and wisdom so that you always remain equal to any situation. For if you give in, if you go spiritually bankrupt, not only will you lose your strength, your security and your authority, but you will also lose all your magnetism and charm, and once these have gone, you will no longer be interesting or attractive to others. Those who fail to understand this are working against their own interests, for once they lose their radiance, people simply abandon them or trample them underfoot.

You must associate with people, you must love them, help them and work with them, but at the same time adhere to your high ideal, to your divine philosophy. In doing so, you become a focal point, a spring, a garden, an orchard for others. Not only will a high ideal fill your every need, but it will also give you the means to help others.

31 March

*O*ne of the essential practices of Christianity is communion. It was not Jesus who instituted this rite; it already existed long before him, for Melchizedek, the high priest of the Almighty, went to meet Abraham bearing bread and wine. Communion is a fundamental act of life and we do not need to wait for a priest to bless the host; we can receive communion every day through the food we eat.

Each one of you can become a high priest – it is our inner calling in the face of the Eternal – and stand before your cells to officiate and give them food and drink. You are a high priest for your cells. If you are conscious of this role, your cells will receive something sacred, and you will sense their joy at being allowed finally to do the work for which they were destined.

1 April

You would like to visit friends but you have no flowers to give them, and the florists are closed. Concentrate for a few minutes with all your love, and imagine the most beautiful fresh flowers – you can even add a card with a few kind words if you wish. After having sent this thought, go to them and you will see how you will be welcomed. Is this how you usually prepare to visit your relatives or friends? No, before going to see them, you brood over grudges you hold against them, already planning how to settle certain scores. So, what good can come of your visit?

You must never visit anyone without bringing them gifts. While you may not be an artist who can paint them pictures, nor a singer or a musician who can sing or play, inwardly, you can always do something. Inwardly, you can do everything: sing, play and bring the finest gifts. This is true magic.

2 April

When two people begin to fall in love, they are content at first to express themselves with a look: then they are drinking water from the high peaks for their love is crystalline and pure. There are no better exchanges than those made with a look.

It is rare, but sometimes we encounter a look that is not of this earth, a divine look replete with a thousand things so subtle that even the greatest poet could not convey what it holds. Of course, for those who prefer concrete, tangible, coarse pleasures, a look means nothing, for they can neither touch it nor hold it in their hands. But there are those for whom a gaze is enough. We can live exclusively on the love such a look expresses.

3 April

Silence is the expression of peace, harmony and perfection. Those who develop a love of silence, and understand that it provides them with the best conditions for psychic and spiritual activity, gradually manage to manifest it in everything they do. Instead of making a commotion when they move objects, when they talk, walk or work, they become more careful, more delicate, more fluid, and everything they do is imbued with something that seems to come from another world, a world of poetry, music, dance and inspiration.

4 April

A seed that has been planted in the ground is just like a creature that has been placed in a tomb. When the angel of warmth appears, it awakens the seed, caresses it and says, 'Go on, get up now and leave this tomb!' And behold! The life that was buried begins to stir. A tiny shoot splits the seed in two and forces its way above ground, giving birth to a stem that will one day grow into a magnificent tree. This is resurrection.

However, there can be no resurrection unless the tomb is opened and only warmth – that is, love – is capable of opening tombs. Those whose hearts are full of love, of selfless, spiritual love, open the tombs of their cells. People have so many cells that are fermenting and falling apart! Indeed, thousands of tiny tombs need to be opened. As long as these cells are not animated and revitalized, they remain dormant, and human beings cannot fathom the inner wealth they possess. But once this resurrection has taken place, once their cells have been awakened, they will no longer be the same, for their consciousness will have expanded. Through everything they feel, everything they experience, they are moving in another dimension, the dimension of the spirit.

5 April

In order to be noticed by an Initiate, a woman presents herself before him with her hair freshly curled, her perfume on, and her make-up in place; every colour is on her face – black, blue, red and green. The Initiate, who has a completely different understanding of beauty, will not tell her that she is mistaken, or that she does not even know to whom she is presenting herself, but he will not be impressed.

Some will say, 'Oh, I see, from now on I will present myself before an Initiate in tatters.' Well, you would be like the proud Athenian who, to gain Socrates' esteem, dressed himself in rags before going to visit him; his skin was even showing through the torn fabric. He stood before Socrates, who looked at him for a long time, then said, 'You see, your pride is still apparent through these holes.' He was not taken in! It does not make much difference whether you wear rags or luxury clothes, because an Initiate looks at your soul.

6 April

Disciples of light never accept anarchy, knowing that if they do, it will first of all take hold deep within them, bringing disorder, imbalance and decay. Even health depends on obedience to a universal order. When we begin to establish this order within us, everything calms down and becomes balanced, harmonized, more attractive, enlightened, strengthened and revived. We then vibrate in unison with the whole cosmos, with all the celestial regions, and we become like a spring, like a sun – something that shines and flows and springs forth.

This is the ideal towards which we should strive instead of leaving a door wide open to all the harmful currents floating about in the form of anarchist philosophies or ideologies. Whether it be an individual, a family, a society or a country, we destroy ourselves when we lay ourselves open to these currents; the law is implacable.

7 *April*

Concentration and meditation are exercises that allow us to gather and store up spiritual energy, which we can use for our work. However, for this exercise to be truly fruitful, you must be able to remain completely still, so as not to make the slightest rustle or creak; first, because the silence must not be disturbed by even the faintest noise, and second, because you lose strength if you are unable to stay absolutely motionless.

Before meditating, move as much as you want, but you must not move a muscle during the meditation, otherwise you will never manage to concentrate your energies on spiritual work.

8 April

*O*nly initiates have learned how to become true children of God. They never leave the Lord to seek independence – they always want to be nourished, educated and protected by Him. Only ignorant and stupid people demand their independence and freedom from the Lord. And then they wonder why they are beset by all kinds of misfortunes. Well, it is not that hard to understand: when we separate ourselves from God, we are no longer protected and supported.

All those who have left their divine parents are weighed down by troubles and burdens. So be like children, and hold on tightly to your heavenly Father and Mother, trust them wholeheartedly.

9 April

You must open yourself up in order to receive the beneficial influences around you. Heaven has poured out all its blessings in abundance and if you fail to receive them, it is because your view of things is so limited that you have cut yourself off from the divine world. Then, you complain, 'Oh, nobody hears me, nobody has come to help me – angels do not exist, God does not exist!' There you have it: human beings create their own deplorable situations, and then they draw conclusions about the existence of God!

They should try to open themselves up a little to heaven, to communicate with divine entities, then they would discover that these entities were there all along to support and enlighten them – it was simply up to them to seek this help. We do ourselves harm when we limit ourselves. So, we must open up, expand ourselves, and then we will be filled with awe, we will feel the divine blessing that is always above and around us.

10 April

You see a man standing there quietly; he is still, with a relaxed expression on his face. Suddenly, he receives a jolt from deep down inside – a thought or a feeling of fear, love or anger – and then everything changes, his features, the look in his eye, the tone of his skin.

How can the physical body change so suddenly under the impulse of something as intangible and subtle as a thought or a feeling? Just one emotion and we become petrified! Sometimes people even die because of an emotion. How can an emotion have such power over the physical body? Everyone has noticed these phenomena, so why haven't they ever drawn the conclusion that the psychic life controls the physical life? The physical body is not responsible for anything; it is always dependent on some element above it that creates, shapes, colours and moulds.

11 April

*A*s a consequence of today's emphasis on developing the intellect, human beings have become aggressive, critical and separate. This is why they are not happy. In order to be happy they must work to develop another principle within themselves: their soul. But the soul can only flourish in the fraternal life where, like bees gathered to make honey, everyone works to realize the will of God and his kingdom on earth.

Once they will have understood the ravages caused by exclusively developing the intellect at the expense of other faculties, human beings will decide to emphasize brotherly relations. Then, they will find happiness.

12 April

*E*ating a lot will not make you healthier. On the contrary, eating a lot is very harmful. What matters is the quality of the food, and above all, the way you eat. Even if you reduce your portions, you can draw more energy from your food if you have learned to absorb it with love and consciousness.

If you manage to free your mind at mealtime and focus your attention on the food so as to penetrate it with rays of love, a separation occurs between its matter and its energy: the matter disintegrates, while the energy enters into you and becomes available to you. The same processes are at work in a thermonuclear plant. If human beings really knew how to eat, only a few mouthfuls would suffice. They would draw enough energy to move the whole universe.

13 April

A Master is like a father or mother who educates you, and just as you must not remain with your father or mother forever, your goal must not be to cling to your Master, but to go towards God. Moreover, your Master does not stay still either, he too goes towards God, and you must follow him to reach God. The point of departure is God, and the destination is also God.

You will say, 'So, my father and mother do not count?' They were like entrepreneurs; they built your body, your house – a cabin or a temple, it depends. 'But I want them to be with me.' Well then, encourage them along your path. But if they do not wish to follow you, you should not stay with them, that is to say, remain at their level. This is why Jesus said, *'You will leave your father and your mother, and you will follow me.'* But he never said to leave your father and mother if they walk with you. How can you leave someone who walks alongside you?

14 April

You always blame the conditions in life and feel that you are the victim of fate, of society, of your family and so on. No, it is you who by your attitude have consciously or unconsciously chosen your present conditions. Change your attitude, and conditions will change. Because they are changing all the time according to the way you are, to your understanding and your behaviour. As long as you think that external, material conditions are the determining factors, and you do nothing to reinforce and improve yourself, know that misfortunes await you. But if you give priority to the spirit, light and inner strength, conditions will eventually conform to these divine principles.

For 'that which is below is like that which is above', and with time, what is above ends up being realized below, in matter.

15 April

*M*any artists have deliberately sought to have multiple love affairs because they believed that love kept their inspiration alive. Unfortunately, this very human, sensual, fickle love, while indeed the source of some inspiration, was principally the cause of tremendous havoc.

Love is like wine, it is intoxicating, but this headiness sought in the lower regions leads to the same physical and moral degeneration as alcohol abuse. And yet knowing how to love is the greatest thing. True love makes you more beautiful, it enlightens you. Thanks to this love, you do good to all creatures, and above all, you are happy. Wisdom will not bring you happiness, neither will power. Power might make you invincible but no happier. To be happy, you have to love.

16 April

*A*lchemists say that to obtain the philosopher's stone, the work must begin when the Sun enters the constellation of Aries and the moon enters that of Taurus, because the Sun is exalted in Aries and the Moon is exalted in Taurus. Gemini, the sign that follows, is ruled by Mercury ☿. The Sun and the Moon unite to give birth to a child, Mercury. The symbol for Mercury is formed by the disc of the Sun and the crescent Moon, with a plus sign +, the sign for addition, to symbolize their union. The symbol for Mercury is thus the union of the Sun and the Moon.

The Sun and the Moon give birth to the child, Mercury, the philosopher's stone. But the philosopher's stone that the alchemists sought was, in reality, a symbol of sublimation, of the transformation of man who becomes luminous, immortal and free. The alchemists worked with the Sun and the Moon, that is to say, with the two principles of will and imagination; and thanks to this work with these two principles, they were able to transform themselves and become like the Sun and the Moon – radiant and pure.

17 April

Human beings no longer hold anything sacred; they have lost their sense of worship. You will say that they try to foster respect for their fellow man. Yes, but that is hardly anything, in fact it is nothing at all. For above and beyond man, there are multitudes of beings whom people neglect and do not even believe in. They hide behind their respect for their 'fellow man' to justify their lack of respect for anything else, even for the Creator himself.

In reality, you cannot truly respect human beings unless you give credence within yourself to something greater. Indeed, you will even do them harm because certain motives operating within you will eliminate this respect. It is only when you harbour a sacred feeling for something, or rather for a greater, more distant being – the Divine – that you will also respect human beings.

18 April

*M*ost human beings cling to their limited concept of life, which is why their face bears the marks of the disarray and turmoil in which they are embroiled. Their lives are nothing but pettiness, discord, arguments and vexations inspired by their lower nature, which they refuse to sacrifice. Yet fire shows us that without sacrifice there would be no life. When you light a fire, all the black, twisted branches are transformed into energy, light and heat. This is why we must make up our mind to light the fire within us in order to burn all the rubbish, which as it is consumed, will also become light and heat.

As long as we equate sacrifice with deprivation and impoverishment, we have not understood a thing. True sacrifice is the transformation of all the worn out, antiquated, impure elements into light and heat, that is, into wisdom and love.

19 April

*I*f you want to improve yourself and become wiser, stronger and more radiant, you must spend a lot of time wishing for and visualizing these qualities. Imagine yourself surrounded by light, sending your love throughout the whole world, and withstanding all temptations and difficulties. Little by little, the images you form of these qualities become alive, they act upon you and transform you as they work to attract the right elements from the universe and draw them into you.

Of course, it takes a good deal of time and work to achieve results, but the day this result presents itself, there can be no doubt about it – you feel a living entity above you protecting you, teaching you, purifying you, enlightening you, and offering you the support you need in times of hardship. You must begin by forming this perfection in the mental realm, and then, it will gradually descend into the material world where it will be realized.

20 April

What characterizes a truly spiritual person and distinguishes them from other people is the extraordinary unity they have achieved within themselves: their thoughts, feelings, and actions are coordinated and directed towards a single ideal; nothing is at odds within them. While in ordinary people, this unity is lacking – their desires pull them in one direction, their thoughts in another, and their actions in yet a third direction.

There is a story about a mole, an eagle and a fish who got together to carry a heavy load. What happened? The mole tried to go underground, the eagle flapped its wings to take flight, and the fish wanted to dive into the water. Obviously, given these competing forces, the load remained exactly where it was! Most human beings also go in all directions, whereas a truly spiritual person's actions are orderly, and directed harmoniously towards a single goal: perfection of a kind that can only be achieved through love, wisdom and the truth.

21 April

Someone presents you with a loaf of bread and says, 'It's really good, it will give you strength.' You take it and eat it, and it makes you sick, so in fact, this bread is bad. The proof is clear – you must not keep eating it. Someone else brings you another loaf of bread, and after having eaten it, you feel great. This proves that their bread is good. The same holds true in every field.

Someone tells you about a philosophy, saying that it is the best, that you should adopt it. Well, do a little checking. If you begin to see more clearly, if you feel more love, impetus, and inspiration in your heart, if your will to work and resolve every problem becomes stronger, then accept this philosophy. Even if a tramp or an outcast presents it to you, it is excellent. You have the proof.

22 April

We must think of purifying ourselves each and every day – yes, every day. You purified yourself yesterday? Well, that was for yesterday; today you must start again. So, start again until your whole being is completely renewed.

Purification is the work of a lifetime. It is not because someone was immersed in water on the day of their baptism that evil spirits will be warded off for the rest of their life. Devils are not afraid of such baptisms! A person must work throughout their life to preserve and nourish what they received on the day of their baptism; if they do not continue to make efforts in the same vein, it is of no use to glory in having been baptized – no trace of it remains.

23 April

Why can human beings not understand that everything they do has consequences and that they cannot continue to transgress the laws of nature and disrupt the work of the elements with impunity?

Through their actions, but also through their thoughts and feelings, and through their anarchic attitude, they provoke the forces of nature, which eventually respond to restore order. Nature is not something lifeless or unfeeling which we have the right to treat as we please. Whenever human beings go beyond the limits of what it can bear, nature strikes back.

24 April

A candle's flame is very small and fragile, a mere breath can blow it out, but if this flame reaches a certain size, then on the contrary, every breath and gust of wind will only increase its power. This image can help you to understand that if you are weak, the least event in life could extinguish your flame, that is to say, your inspiration and your impetus. But if you are strong, this flame will become a blaze that difficulties and obstacles will only fuel.

As long as little things can strike you down, your flame is very weak. So gather more branches to feed it. You will say, 'But I do not have any!' What do you mean you have no branches? Sacrifice all the old wood, those black branches and old things you have inside you – your baser instincts and desires – throw them into the fire. Not only will you be rid of them, but never again will anything or anyone be able to extinguish the blaze burning within you.

25 April

*H*ow can we become a gemstone? How can we become a diamond? Originally, a diamond is just carbon – ugly, black carbon – that is transformed under the effects of tremendous pressure and extremely high temperature.

Well, it could be said that the tale of a diamond is that of an Initiate. He too was simple carbon at first, but thanks to the enormous pressure he had to withstand (his trials) and the high temperature he has borne within him (his love), he has become a diamond, a pure, sparkling light, and he is now set on the crown of an angel, an archangel or a divinity.

26 April

The region of true thought is the causal plane, that is, the higher mental plane, and the further thought strays from these heights, the more it is obstructed and diverted. Yet, in order to face all the problems of everyday life with which human beings are confronted, their thought is forced to descend and clothe itself in thick, coarse garments. Dressed this way, thought becomes unrecognizable and loses its power.

Thought is all-powerful on high. Once it descends to the level of the intellect (the lower mental plane) and the heart (the astral plane), it gets covered in grime, and as it is no longer as pure, it loses almost all its penetrative strength. If you want your thought to regain its true power, its ability to meditate and to unite you with heaven, you must rise up to the causal plane.

* See plate and note on p. 396 and 397.

27 April

*T*hanks to their intellectual faculties, human beings have made colossal achievements in the physical realm. We cannot fail to see how scientific and technical progress has transformed life, but this is not enough.

Humanity is now called upon to realize even greater achievements, by means of the faculties of the spirit. Through meditation and prayer, they must learn to build a relationship with the world of the spirit, so that the light, love and power of the spirit may descend upon the earth, inside them, and upon those beings around them. Technical progress has limits, and even poses danger if it is not made to serve a higher vision of things. We therefore need to go further, and it is by means of the spirit that life will be truly transformed, because peace, freedom and brotherhood are realizations of the spirit.

28 April

*T*he creatures of the divine world love and respect only those who are rich. If you want to attract the attention of the entities of light and the forces of nature, you have to be wealthy, because not only will they give nothing to the poor, they will even take away what the poor have. They give to those who already have, and take from the have-nots what little they possess.

In fact, in France, there is a proverb that says 'lend only to the rich'. People have never really understood the meaning or origins of this truth; they find it cruel and unfair. Why give to the person who already has and take from the other what little they still have left? Well no, it is completely fair – heaven gives its blessings to those who have acquired spiritual wealth, whereas those who are spiritually poor and have done nothing to increase their wealth eventually lose what little they had.

29 April

You can find everything in the universe – heaven, earth and even hell – it is up to you to know where you want to go. If you have wandered carelessly into hell, that is no reason to linger there forever, you can leave. It may happen that you have to go to the bistro for a drink with friends, but this does not mean that you should never leave the bistro. You go for a walk in the forest and wish to gather strawberries; this is fine, but think about returning home, or night will fall and you will not be able to find your way back. You may have said some unfortunate words and made a mess of things. It does not matter, now speak words of a different kind and make it right! And if you fall into a swamp infested with bugs that sting you, instead of shouting and saying your prayers, hurry out and move somewhere more hospitable.

Even in the worst situations, remember that nothing is final and that we must only think to remove ourselves or to make amends.

30 April

Whatever you undertake, first ask yourself, 'I seek light, I seek love, I seek true power – will I find them by doing this or that?' Thanks to Initiatic Science, you can get the correct answer right away. Otherwise, you will throw yourself body and soul into endeavours that will gradually weaken and destroy you.

Look at businessmen who are always agitated and race the world over to find yet another market, to open yet another branch. How many of them realize that all these responsibilities and activities through which they set out to satisfy their greed will destroy their nervous system, which soon will no longer be able to cope with these stresses? They lose sleep, they lose their peace of mind, and they lose their health. So, what benefits will they gain from all this? Before setting out to acquire something, or before taking on a certain role or position, it is important to know where this desire will eventually lead you.

1 May

The highest ideal is to model oneself on the sun: its life, warmth and light. If your model is a scholar, a writer, a philosopher, or even a hero or a saint, you will no doubt be influenced by their qualities and virtues, but there will always be something missing. Even if you take the greatest masters of humanity as your model, you will still not have an image of true perfection.

The image of perfection is the sun; and if, in the desire to give light, warmth and life to creatures, you take the sun as your model, you yourself will be transformed. For even if you never obtain the sun's light, warmth and life, the very desire to acquire them will propel you to the celestial regions where you will truly accomplish marvels. Your desire to give light, warmth and life will make you more luminous, warmer and more alive.

2 May

*D*oes everyone have to be a lawyer, a philosopher or a scholar to join in a revolution, a strike or a street demonstration? No, but all must be present and united as one – the learned and the ignorant, the skilled and the unskilled, the weak and the strong – so as to emerge victorious! We see this kind of thing in the newspapers and on television every day, but we have not managed to interpret it. 'But what is there to understand?' you will ask. Many things, but in particular the quantity of people gathered to make demands is what gets results, not the quality. The fact that there are drunkards and invalids in the crowd is of secondary importance. What matters is that even those drunkards and invalids join forces with all the others in their claim for change.

And what is important here, when it comes to asking for the kingdom of God? Of course, we must make every effort to be good, upright and disinterested, yes. But, above all, we must all want to join together so that the clamour of a huge crowd of human beings asking for the kingdom of God may be heard.

3 May

When Jesus said to his disciples, *'If you have faith the size of a mustard seed, you will say to this mountain' "Move from here to there," and it will move'*, of course, this mountain is symbolic. It represents the great difficulties in life that only faith enables us to move, that is to say, to resolve. We can move these mountains stone by stone in one year, two years, ten years. You think that this is too long and you would like it to be done right away. Well, in that case, you must work like ants who in no time are able to transport real mountains of grain – proportionally, they are mountains to them! Yes, but an ant does not work alone, masses of them work together.

Isolation and selfishness will never enable us to move mountains. If great things have been achieved over the course of history, it is because men and women joined forces to work together. To move mountains is to tear down the obstacles within ourselves and in the world that are opposed to the coming of the kingdom of God.

4 May

*G*et into the habit of saying 'thank you'. Yes, give thanks every minute of the day, and in every circumstance. Never stop giving thanks, even in the midst of difficulties, sorrow and suffering, for this neutralizes the poisons and heals the wounds caused by these negative states – nothing can resist gratitude. So, give thanks until you feel that everything that happens to you is for your own good. From now on, say, 'Thank you, Lord, thank you, Lord'.

Give thanks for what you do have, but also for what you do not have; for the things that delight you and for those that make you suffer. This is how you will keep the flame of life burning within you. I see that you are thinking, 'Is that all there is to it?' Yes, that is all, but practice this method and you will see the results.

5 May

People who are ruled by their passions are like a primeval earth, always in turmoil and chaos. Of course, life still manages to sustain itself amidst all these upheavals, but the conditions are not conducive for it to produce very elaborate forms. The unleashing of passions puts human beings in a state that is incompatible with the emergence of a culture, a civilization. Passionate man remains a world in the grip of chaos; it is only when this primitive world becomes more peaceful and organized, that plants, animals and human beings will begin to dwell there, and life in the true sense of the word can finally exist.

This is why the Initiates give us warnings and advice: so that we may learn to prepare a world within us in which even angels and divinities can dwell in the form of inspiration, intuition and revelations that will make us truly happy.

6 May

*T*he Scriptures say, *'Whatever you bind on earth will be bound in heaven, and whatever you loose on earth, will be loosed in heaven.'* These words are extraordinarily significant. Whether you are aware of it or not, what you do below on the physical plane is reflected above on the subtle planes. When you bind someone on the physical plane, you bind him on the astral and mental planes*. When you release someone on the physical plane, you release him on the astral and mental planes.

When a mother has to leave her infant alone for a moment in its pram, she straps it in so that it cannot fall out. The infant is bound on the physical plane, but it is bound on the astral plane as well; it does not feel free, so it cries. When the mother comes back and frees her child on the physical plane, it is all smiles again because she has also freed it on the astral plane. If you lock someone in a dungeon and deprive him of food, he will also feel limited on the astral and mental planes, and he will suffer and be unhappy. In fact, there are all sorts of ways of binding people or releasing them from their constraints by means of words, a look, a gesture, and so on.

* See plate and note on p. 396 and 397.

7 May

When we study human beings, we see that everything within them makes demands – the stomach asks for food; the ears ask for sounds; the eyes ask for light and colour; and the mouth, nose, and sexual organs all ask for something too. So, the whole body makes demands, which is wonderful, marvellous and natural. But there must be a head in charge of all these demands to see if it can satisfy them, otherwise there will be chaos. People will eat and drink too much or not enough, they will overexpose themselves to heat or cold; they will not hear or see the dangers.

So, it is good that the body clamours for what it needs, but only as long as the head is there to guide it, and decide when to accept, when to refuse and how much to give. Demands and requests come from all sides, but the head must always be there, in order to distribute everything according to divine rules and proportions.

8 May

In response to a question he was asked, Master Peter Deunov once said you could tell what a person's degree of evolution was by the intensity of the light emanating from them.

I was very young at the time, I did not yet have these criteria and this reply made such a deep impression on me that from then on it became the foundation of a large part of my existence. Throughout my life, I too have seen that we could judge people by their light. Of course, this light is not actually visible, but one can sense it in the way a person looks at you, in their facial expression and in the harmony of their gestures. This light does not depend on intellectual faculties or education; it is a manifestation of divine life. It is this light we must seek, without ever feeling that we have had enough.

9 May

Hierarchy is an order on an ascending scale in which not only are the lower elements subject to the higher ones, but in which the actions of the different elements converge towards a summit, towards a centre. This idea of convergence is essential. Take the case of a tree; where is its head? You will say that it is the top. No, the head of a tree is its roots through which it receives life. In relation to human beings, a tree is upside down – its head is buried under the earth. If the branches, leaves, flowers and fruits are not connected to the roots, the tree withers and dies. This is the image used by Jesus in the parable of the vine, *'I am the vine and you are the branches. Those who abide in me and I in them bear much fruit, because apart from me you can do nothing.'*

A hierarchy also exists in man, from the feet all the way up to the brain. The whole can be harmonious and well balanced only if all the organs cooperate and strive towards the same goal, in obedience to the one preeminent central principle, the spirit. This is the only way to achieve unity, and unity is the primary basis for life.

10 May

*E*ven if science continues to invent more and more ways of making life easier – and indeed, it will – human beings must not stop making efforts. If it becomes easier for them to act upon exterior material, so much the better! However, they should then devote a little more of their free time to working on their inner matter, to mastering and spiritualizing it, so as to perfect themselves and become a beneficial presence for the whole world. With every effort, with every exercise, life takes on another colour, another flavour.

So many people who have everything in life are so jaded that they no longer feel anything! Yes, because there is absolutely no activity going on inside, no intensity to their life. If they were enlightened, they would continue to take advantage of all the material possibilities without ceasing their inner work. Because it is this work that gives everything its flavour.

11 May

*H*ope, faith and love – these three virtues correspond respectively to form, content and meaning. Hope is linked to form, faith to content and love to meaning. It is the form that prepares and preserves the content. The content brings strength, and strength has no reason for being without meaning.

Hope affects the physical body. When it is strong, it has a beneficial influence on the stomach, liver and intestines; if, on the contrary, it is weak or lacking, it has an adverse effect both on the digestive system and on the beauty of the body.

Faith, which corresponds to the content, is linked to strength. If you want to have plenty of energy and live life to the full, you must cultivate faith.

And it is love that gives the deepest and fullest meaning to life. However learned and wealthy we may be, if love does not flow through our being like a spring, life will have no meaning.

12 May

*H*uman beings do not particularly enjoy hearing about fidelity and stability. They find it boring; they need change. But who says that stability and faithfulness are incompatible with change? We can vary anything we like as long as we do not change direction.

Masters and initiates also like change and variety, but not just anywhere or anyhow. A Master is in favour of outer variety, and inner unity, that is to say fidelity to a high ideal.

13 May

Matter is the form that contains, confines, and compresses the spirit. An atomic explosion for example is actually the spirit erupting in the form of heat and fire. For the explosion to happen, the spirit must be compressed within matter, for of itself matter can do nothing, it is no more than a support, a container.

This is why people are mistaken when they marvel at the power of matter. They fail to see that the forces released from it are the forces of the spirit, which are only stored there for a while to be kept safe until the time comes for them to manifest themselves. The proof is that once these forces have been released, they cannot be recovered. Once the spirit has escaped, it is impossible to recapture it; it returns to the regions from which it came. As for matter, there is nothing left of it, it is pulverized, annihilated by the spirit.

14 May

When you wake up in the morning, you are born on the physical plane but you die on the astral plane, and in the evening when you go to sleep, you die on the physical plane but you are born on the astral plane.

Similarly, when a child comes into the world, it is born here but it dies on the other side. It is welcomed here with songs and music, while its funeral procession is taking place on the other side. Conversely, when a person dies here, they are accompanied to the grave with funeral marches and the tears of black-clad mourners, while on the other side they are greeted with fanfares, as those who receive them exclaim, 'At last, he has returned!' Of course, if a person has behaved badly on earth, they will not receive such a warm welcome over there, just as children are not always met with great rejoicing by their parents here. But these are secondary details. The law is true: life in one region is death in another; that which disappears here, appears elsewhere, and vice versa.

15 May

A human being can be compared to a tree.

The roots correspond to the stomach and sexual organs, for human beings are rooted in the earth by means of their stomach, which enables them to nourish themselves, and by their sexual organs, which enable them to reproduce.

The trunk is represented by the lungs and the heart, that is to say, the respiratory system and the arterial and venous system through which the blood circulates. The elaborated sap flows down to nourish the tree, while the upward flow carries the raw sap to the leaves where it is transformed. The same principle is at work in our bloodstream, whereby the arteries carry the clean, pure blood, and the veins carry the tainted blood.

The leaves, flowers and fruit of a tree correspond to the head. All our thoughts represent our fruit because it is through the mind that a human being bears fruit.

16 May

God has given inertia to matter and impetus to the spirit, and human beings are placed between the two. They are outwardly covered with matter, but the spirit dwells within them. This means that they are subject to a twofold influence: at times they are animated by the spirit, and at others, matter tries to engulf them and drag them back to primeval chaos.

Humans must constantly struggle to remain inwardly active so that the currents may flow; if they give in to inertia they become a swamp. This is what happens to people who do no intellectual, spiritual or divine work – they become foul-smelling bogs infested with tadpoles, frogs and bugs. Whereas those who are enlightened, well directed and guided not only take care never to repress the spirit, but open all their doors to it. And once the spirit is king, it begins to pacify, harmonize, vivify and illuminate the whole of their being.

17 May

In the spiritual life, you must not be concerned with time. If you set yourself a deadline to overcome this failing or achieve that inner result, you will succeed only in becoming tense and you will not develop in a harmonious manner.

You must work towards perfection without setting any time limit, knowing that eternity lies before you and that sooner or later you will attain the perfection you long for. Your only thought should be for the beauty of the work you have undertaken. Tell yourself, 'Since it is so beautiful, I need not worry about whether it will take me hundreds or thousands of years to complete: I am working, that is all.'

18 May

*I*f your one desire is to settle yourself comfortably on earth, you will be obliged to bury yourself in matter, that is to say, to burden yourself with more and more responsibilities, commitments and relationships, and you will not have a minute left to breathe, to reflect and to meditate.

All those who think of nothing but expanding their territory and opening branches everywhere to make as much money as possible, end up being crushed by the weight of it all; and even if you want to go and look for them under the rubble, they are nowhere to be found. They have submerged themselves thousands of miles below ground and although they call for help, reaching their hand out to you, there is nothing you can do for them. This is where their materialistic philosophy has put them! Oh, of course, they are successful, everybody congratulates them – or rather idiots congratulate them, and not only do they congratulate them but they want to be just like them, buried, unable to breathe or see the sky. Yes, unfortunately, this is how the majority of human beings understand life.

19 May

Never let your inner states of discomfort reach such proportions that you can no longer remedy them.

Here is an image: If you step carelessly in wet cement and are so lost in thought that you neglect to remove your feet, the cement will set. It will even become so hard that you will find yourself trapped. Someone will have to go and get some tools to break the cement and you might be hurt in the process. Well, this is what happens in the inner life. If we fail to remedy certain mistakes and shortcomings quickly, soon it is too late – the repairs are very expensive and may well cause further damage.

20 May

Clairvoyance is generally associated with the element water. The book of Genesis says that God separated the waters above from the waters below. The waters above represent the cosmic library in which the archives of the universe are kept. This library, referred to in the esoteric tradition as the Akasha Chronica, bears the imprints left by every creature that has ever existed and of every event that has ever taken place on earth since the beginning of time.

This is why some clairvoyants work with water; they stare into a bowl of water in order to 'see'. It is not that they actually see anything in the water, but through it, they make contact with the waters above and with the images floating in those waters. In this way, their spirit finds what they are looking for.

21 May

A mantra, a sacred formula is like a mould that must be filled with intense life, that is to say, with love and faith. When a formula is spoken out loud, it sets in motion currents that rise through the heavenly hierarchies up to the throne of God. A formula must always be pronounced at least three times in order to reach the three worlds – physical, spiritual and divine*. Tireless repetition of the same formula penetrates the depth of the subconscious where the roots of our being lie, and it is there, in the roots of our being, that we have great possibilities of transformation.

It is important to pronounce the formulas aloud because sound is extremely powerful on the physical plane. If you think a formula without saying it, its forces accumulate only on the mental plane and nothing happens on the physical plane. The spoken word is necessary in order to give invisible forces the power to act.

* See plate and note on p. 396 and 397.

22 May

*S*ympathy and antipathy are natural feelings that even sages experience. However, the difference between a sage and an ordinary person is that a sage surmounts their antipathy and does not give in blindly to their sympathies.

Our actions must not be determined by sympathy or antipathy because these are often personal feelings that stem from experiences lived in previous incarnations with beings whom we meet again in this life. They do not provide impartial information about a person's true worth, their qualities or their flaws. We have to learn how to do things we do not enjoy, and not only show kindness to people we dislike, but also try to see the errors and shortcomings of those we do like.

23 May

Life is never the same: it ebbs and flows, ever changing, moving us and everything else about. Today, we may feel justly proud because we have managed to solve a problem, but tomorrow another development may arise which cannot be tackled with the same methods and approach – we are obliged to adapt to this new situation. Know that life will always present us with different problems to resolve, and we need to find a specific solution for each one. For example, yesterday a good deed or a generous gesture may have been the answer, but today another difficulty presents itself, perhaps requiring the solution of reason, or action, or patience – or even by turning a deaf ear. So, always try to find how best to adapt to every problem.

24 May

*U*ntil people choose to use spiritual strength and the power of divine love to solve their problems, things will never get any better. The proof is that we hear only talk of armaments these days. In order to achieve military superiority, every country is busy developing increasingly lethal weapons, until one day, should they use them, they will destroy the whole earth. With this approach, the more time passes, the more complicated things become.

As of today, try to resolve all your problems with family, friends and enemies by manifesting love and kindness. By doing so, you set in motion a law that will eventually oblige them to respond in kind. Yes, this is the power of provocation. Until you understand how you can solve your problems, you will continue to provoke other people's worst side – always their worst side – and that worst side lies there in wait for you to drop your guard, for you to weaken, and then it strikes back. Study history, this has always been the case.

25 May

Philosophers never tire of debating the question of whether or not man is free. Some think that he is, others think that he is not, but in fact, they are not asking the right question. Freedom is not a condition that is given or withheld from man once and for all. Man's freedom with respect to the present is very limited, because the present is the consequence of a past and it is impossible to go back and change it; we must put up with the past, and digest it. It is with respect to the future that we are free, because we have the means to create the future we wish for.

It is essential that we grasp this truth so that we may know how to orientate our work. Once we know we can do something to improve the future, we no longer suffer the present, and we prepare ourselves to become even greater masters of our own destiny.

26 May

No book can teach you more essential truths than the Gospels. You will say that you have read them and have not discovered much in them, which is why you are now turning towards oriental teachings. Well, this simply proves that you have not understood the immeasurable wisdom contained in these Gospels that were written for you. Yes, I know, people have had their fill of these texts they know so well, and they want a change of diet, but it is dangerous to go searching for it in teachings that are not destined for you, that are not designed for your structure or your mentality.

The teaching that was designed for Westerners is that of Christ. You have not read it seriously or meditated on it. You are genuinely searching for something, I know, but to what end? Very often, people follow an oriental teaching in order to brag about it or simply to be different, but that is pointless. It only proves that they like the outlandish and not the simple truth.

27 May

*H*earing and sight leave human beings free, whereas smell, taste and touch enslave them, for they require them to be in close contact with objects and other beings. The sad thing is that the higher senses – sight and hearing – often encourage people to use the lower senses; yes, the eyes and ears try their utmost to sign contracts with the nose, mouth and hands.

A man who marvels at a woman's beauty and the sound of her voice is not content to just look and listen, he will go to great lengths to get close enough to breathe in her perfume, caress her and embrace her. Disciples understand that they must break this contract, that they must stop trying to get physically close to people and things in order to smell, taste and touch them, but remain only in contact with their subtle dimension by means of their ears and eyes.

28 May

*S*uppose that during a conversation with your boss or a colleague, you were not really paying attention and you let slip a few unfortunate words. Well that does it, the relationship is finished, you are fired, and then there are lawsuits, expenses and so forth. You say that you will make amends, but that is also a costly business. So, try to understand that it is always to your advantage to be watchful and sensible so as not to complicate things, at least within yourself to begin with.

Outwardly, of course, there will always be disorder and conflict, we cannot change the world; but in all that we do ourselves, it is possible, if we are conscious and vigilant, to introduce harmony, peace and light. If you work patiently every day, things will eventually work out for you, even on the material plane. By your conduct, you will earn the esteem and friendship of those around you, and everyone will want to help you, and do good things for you. Yes, with care and wisdom we can solve many problems.

You still do not know what hope really is. Hope is a wisdom that knows how to use the past and the present in order to shape the future. Hope is the ability to live a magnificent reality that has not yet come about on the physical plane. Hope is a foretaste of perfection. Thanks to hope, you can eat and drink a happiness that you do not yet possess, but which is the true reality. For true reality is not on the physical plane, it is in the divine world.

The true reality is that you are heirs to heaven and earth. Your inheritance is there, but as you are still too young, you cannot yet take possession of it; but your inheritance is waiting for you.

30 May

*D*uring the waxing moon, the physical and psychic energies that nature has placed in you help you to manifest yourself as a conscious, active, and strong-willed being. Then, during the fourteen days of the waning moon, you will find that these energies tend to withdraw so as to nourish your roots, that is to say, the stomach and sexual organs. Your appetite and sensuality are heightened and you need more rest.

Since these alternations exist, we should know how to make use of them. For example, it is better not to launch a new enterprise while the moon is on the wane, for it is more likely to fail or meet with major obstacles. On the other hand, if you want to rid yourself of a weakness, a vice, a sorrow, or a mental torment, you can take advantage of this period and say, 'As the moon wanes in the sky, so too may such and such a weakness within me wane and disappear.' Conversely, while the moon is waxing, you can pronounce formulas to reinforce your qualities and succeed in your undertakings.

31 May

*T*he reason why many people find it so difficult to practice spiritual exercises is that they do not know how to establish the right inner attitude. There they are, in a hurry, tense at the thought of the million and one other things they have to do, so they are unable to set all these concerns aside. In their unconscious, in their subconscious, there is something that hinders them and prevents them from getting results.

Obviously, the hectic pace of life today and the many obligations it imposes are not conducive to spiritual activities, which require us to know how to free ourselves from our daily cares and adopt a different rhythm. But those who get into the habit of devoting half an hour or an hour to achieving certain conditions of inner peace, will not only find that they are able to meditate, but that they can carry out all their professional and family obligations more easily. There is a time and place for everything.

1 June

Men and women blithely enter into relationships or marriage, imagining that everything is going to be easy, carefree and agreeable. Then, little by little, they feel themselves boxed in, and the arguments and bickering begin, until they realize that if they want their relationship to work, they will have to make an effort to think less about themselves and more about each other.

What they mistook for a playground is in fact a school where the most important apprenticeship for every human being begins: expanding one's consciousness. Do you wonder what this growth in consciousness involves? It means breaking out of one's small, limited self in order to enter the immense community of beings.

2 June

*I*t is good to find opportunities to exercise self-control, for example by learning to endure hunger, thirst, heat, cold or fatigue. This is not to say you should constantly live in a state of deprivation or become yogis. No, of course not. But look how people generally rush to find something to eat or drink the moment they are hungry or thirsty, and if they do not find it immediately, they complain, grumble and become angry.

Observe yourselves and you will see that in all kinds of situations, you cannot bear being unable to satisfy your desires and even your petty whims at once. So how are you going to control your anger, your jealousy, your hatred or your sexual desires? You may well know that it is best to control yourself and you may have tried to do so, but if you haven't learned to exercise your willpower, you will not succeed.

3 June

The water we know and use every day to wash ourselves is a materialization of the cosmic fluid that fills all of space. By means of thought, it is possible to establish a relationship with this fluid and to purify ourselves upon contact with it.

The first step is to wash yourself with the awareness that through this physical water you are touching an element of a spiritual nature. Therefore, try to wash yourself using measured, harmonious gestures, so that your thought may free itself too and do its work. Concentrate on the water, on how cool, clear and pure it is, and you will soon feel that it is reaching unknown regions within you and producing transformations there. Not only will you feel lighter and purified, but your heart and intellect will also be nourished by new, subtler and more life-giving elements. Physical water contains all the elements and forces of spiritual water; you just have to learn to awaken them in order to receive them.

4 June

The best way to link yourself with God during meditation is to work with light, for light is the expression of divine splendour. You must concentrate on light and work with it, steep yourself in it and delight in it.

It is by way of light that we enter into relationship with God. Light is like an ocean of pulsating, vibrating life; you can dive into it to swim, purify yourself, drink, and nourish yourself. It is in light that you will find fulfilment.

5 June

The goal of initiation is to release human beings from the limited sphere of their lower selves and to enable them to reach the limitless region of cosmic consciousness which dwells within them, but of which they have as yet no clear knowledge.

There are thus two poles: yourself, here – the consciousness you have of yourself, in other words, your lower self – and your sublime Self, which also lives within you, which works and manifests itself without your being fully conscious of it. You can imagine this sublime Being who wants to know itself through the dense matter of your being. It already knows itself on high, to be sure, but it wants to know itself through you, through opaque matter. This effort you make to imagine your higher Self coming closer will one day result in such an illumination that your consciousness will know no more limits. You will dwell in the light and will finally feel at one with your higher Self.

6 June

When human beings neglect their ties to the divine world, they cut themselves off from their true roots and lose all sense of the meaning of life. The divine world is not like an external, foreign country that you can ignore with impunity. The divine world is your own inner earth, the world of your soul and spirit, and by cutting your ties with it, you deprive yourself of the resources you most need to live.

When faced with life's ordeals and problems, some people instinctively turn again to this higher reality. But this isn't enough. It is in every moment of daily life that human beings must be conscious of this rich and powerful world within, where they can endlessly draw spiritual resources such as strength, courage, inspiration and so forth.

7 June

*I*t is fear that drives animals to become watchful, cunning and intelligent. But obviously, the form of intelligence that fear develops in creatures is a faculty very low down on the evolutionary ladder. Nature found this to be good for animals, but it is different where human beings are concerned; nature has planned another form of intelligence for them.

If human beings become vigilant and intelligent out of fear – fear of losing their money, their home, their health, their job or their good name – they as yet possess only an animal form of intelligence. But since it is their mission to go further than animals, another emotion must arise in them to replace fear, and this emotion is love. Love drives out fear. When love motivates human beings, true intelligence, divine intelligence, begins to awaken in them.

8 June

As soon as you realize that you have taken a wrong turn, that in succumbing to the lure of fleeting pleasures you have been serving negative forces, turn back, and quickly distance yourself from these dangerous regions where you lost your way. Understand that your entire future depends on the regions toward which you are heading.

Religion teaches that God punishes us for our evil deeds and rewards us for our good ones. But this is simply a manner of presenting things. The truth is that God neither punishes nor rewards us. It is we ourselves, by our thoughts, feelings and actions, who choose to enter this or that region within us; and depending on our choice, either we have to suffer or else we benefit from those regions with splendid conditions. There is an enormous difference between heading into regions of light and those of darkness!

9 June

*T*he sun's rays are powerful forces and wherever they penetrate, they produce great transformations. Entities inhabit these rays and manifest themselves differently depending on their colour – red, blue, green, yellow, and so on. When these rays are projected onto living beings, they carry out a great deal of work on them. Initiates make use of light and colours to help human beings, and they also teach their disciples to work with light.

There are seven colours, and to each of them corresponds a virtue. This is why you must understand that each fault you commit weakens the power within you that corresponds to one of these colours. From the beginning of time, the true initiates have worked with light, for light alone can give you true power, true knowledge. With the advent of the laser, official science is gradually discovering the extraordinary power of light, but far greater still are the powers of spiritual light.

10 June

All the great Masters, all the great initiates teach us that man is a spirit, a flame issuing, like the earth itself, from the heart of the Eternal. Human beings have a long road to travel, and along the way, like the earth, they too may allow themselves to grow lifeless, cold and dark. But they are destined to return to the regions they once left, and one day, after a great deal of time, after many, many incarnations, just as the earth will become like the sun, human beings will return to their heavenly Father. The laws and correspondences are the same for both.

11 June

You can criticize the philosophy of materialists, but you cannot deny their good work. These people are real heroes! They have taken upon themselves the tremendous burden of working with matter, and they are energetic, enterprising and audacious. They are able to do all kinds of things that mystics and contemplatives cannot do.

However, these remarks are not to be taken as encouragement to desert the spiritualists' camp to go and swell the ranks of the materialists. It is good to carry out work on earth, but it would be a mistake to imagine that only the earth exists. And when materialists arrive in the next world, they will find themselves completely at a loss, because they will have worked only for the earth. So here is the best solution: become an idealist when it comes to philosophy and a materialist when it comes to work in order to be a good worker in the field of matter. In other words, know both how to think well and act well.

12 June

Sorrow, unhappiness and discouragement are impurities you have allowed within you and which upset your psychic organism, just as poison and other toxic substances upset your physical organism.

If you learn to use the powers of water, you can remedy these states. Look at water flow, listen to it – whether a spring, a stream or a waterfall, running water frees the solar plexus by carrying off the dark elements that disturbed it. For flowing water is an image of the perpetual renewal of life, and by watching it flow we are influenced by it. Of course, in the city, it is not always easy to come across springs or waterfalls in everyday life but you can always turn on a tap! It is less poetic but it can be just as effective. What matters is to concentrate on flowing water.

13 June

Sensibility is a sign of evolution. The more a person's sensibility increases, the more the life they receive becomes intense and abundant. When people's sensibility diminishes, they regress toward the level of animals, plants and stones. You will say that the more sensitive you are, the more vulnerable you are to suffering. That is true, but even if it entails greater suffering, it is preferable to increase your sensibility, for in doing so you enhance the intensity of your life.

As for those who possess this sensibility, they must be careful to practice moderation in order not to lose it, for excesses dull sensibility. If you read too much, for instance, your brain becomes saturated and you lose your taste for reflection. In order to understand what is most essential, you must not let too many ideas accumulate in your head. And where friendship and love are concerned, we must also remain vigilant and maintain a certain distance. Those who plunge headlong into the effervescence of love end by becoming jaded – they no longer feel anything. Sensibility develops in those who know how to reduce quantity and increase quality.

14 June

*A*ll plant life on earth, including the fruit and vegetables we eat, is impregnated with negative forces. The earth is one vast cemetery, watered by the blood of human beings and steeped in their crimes. And since those who cultivate the fields and gardens often work without love and in a state of inner rebellion, their thoughts and feelings penetrate the seeds they sow, which then poison the earth and its fruits.

How beneficial it would now be to rediscover the art of cultivating the earth according to initiatic rules! These rules, which were known and respected in certain civilizations of the past, concern working with cosmic energies so that when scattered in the soil, seeds capture these energies and impart to the earth's fruits the greatest possible nutritional and curative virtues.

Thought is made of an extremely subtle matter that has the ability to travel through space faster than the speed of light. This means we are able to use it to capture elements in the universe, to visit the sun, to connect with heavenly entities, to draw strength and light from them and to receive revelations.

If you accustom your thought to do this work every day, you will feel that you are truly beginning to live the divine life.

16 June

*A*ll our illnesses, whatever they may be, stem from foreign elements that we have allowed to enter us, to penetrate our physical and psychic organisms. And because these elements are foreign, they create disorder. We only need to drive them out and order is fully restored.

This is why purity is so important for human beings' mental and physical health – purity, that is to say, the rejection of any element that interferes with the proper functioning of our organism. Unfortunately, as soon as human beings hear the word purity, they turn a deaf ear. For them, purity is a narrow, old-fashioned notion fit only for convents, so they continue to swallow anything that comes along: indigestible food, polluted air, dark thoughts and chaotic feelings. When will they understand that it is these impurities that create so many problems for them? If they worked on purity, they would be healthier, more intelligent, wiser and stronger.

17 June

The ancients knew how to penetrate the secrets of nature. Stopping by a spring, for example, they would remain there a long while, watching it flow, so alive, limpid and fresh, and listening to it murmur. In doing so, they gradually made contact with the water's soul, with the spring's soul. And they did the same with fire, the sky, and trees – they listened, they contemplated.

And you too must become attentive to the language of nature. Even if you feel that you understand nothing, it doesn't matter. What matters is that you open yourself up, for in this way you prepare the subtle centres that will one day bring you into contact with living nature.

18 June

So many people endlessly complain that they lack this, that someone owes them that, that no one loves them or thinks of them, that others are ill intentioned and so on. But why don't they realize that their egotism and unreasonable demands put off everyone around them? They need to be helped, supported, rescued, this is true, but they must realize that this very selfish pursuit of happiness will get them nowhere.

Those who think only of getting more for themselves, who imagine the whole world should revolve around them, are setting themselves up for a life of disappointment and suffering. In order to be happy, you must become a servant.

19 June

*O*bserve yourself when you love someone: the mere presence of this feeling inside you makes you think and behave in a certain way, and not just towards the person you love. Because of this feeling, your relationships with everyone around you and even with nature are different.

Love is a force that acts on you, on your mind, on your will and even on your body; it gives you immense possibilities. Love is like fuel: if there is fuel in your car, you can drive. But if you lack fuel, where can you go?

20 June

Artists create works of art that are external to themselves using material that is external to themselves; and as it is on this outer material that they concentrate their efforts, even if they produce masterpieces, when we meet these artists, we find that they themselves are not so magnificent. Often, we are astounded – their behaviour and their attitude are completely devoid of all the beauty found in their creations. They express neither balance, nor harmony, nor poetry.

Well, understand that for initiates, true artists are those who are able to use themselves as the material for their creations. All the methods of the spiritual life are there at our disposal to help and inspire us in this endeavour. Yes, it is first and foremost within ourselves that we must create music and poetry, harmonious forms and movements, and shimmering colours. You will say, 'But no one will see or hear anything!' That is true; people will neither see nor hear this harmony in the way they see and hear classic art forms, but those around you will sense it and benefit from it.

21 June

The true roots of matter are on high, close to God. They are the four holy living creatures, the Seraphim. This means that matter is of divine origin, but at this degree of purity and subtlety, it is unknowable and inconceivable, for it is one with the spirit.

However, since discoveries in physics are revealing ever-subtler forms of matter, perhaps physicists will eventually develop instruments capable of observing the structure and movements of etheric matter. As for astral and mental matter*, it is of course unthinkable; we can only work with them. In fact, we do work with them; you all work with them, but unconsciously. Your thoughts, feelings and states of consciousness are all material processes, but they are so subtle that their projections, the material movements they produce remain imperceptible.

* See plate and note on p. 396 and 397.

22 June

Where music is concerned, it is not so much our intellectual understanding that matters, as the feelings aroused in us by the sounds, vibrations and harmonies. Do we understand the song of birds, of running water, or of the wind in the branches? No, but they captivate us and fill us with wonder. It is always better to sing songs in their original language: even if you do not understand them, there is a special relationship between the words and the music, and translation destroys this relationship.

Music is not made to be understood, but to be felt. Even when it is accompanied by words, it is what we feel that is most important. Of course, it is even better if the two – understanding and feeling – go hand in hand, but it is our feeling that matters most.

23 June

Jesus said, *'Unless you die you shall not live.'*
This means that if we do not die to our lower,
instinctual, animal life, we will never live the
higher life, the life of God himself. We must
surrender our place to the Lord so that He may
come to reign within us and organize everything,
for He alone is wise, powerful and all loving.

Imagine you are melting into infinite space,
into the universal Soul, and ask the Lord to come
and dwell within you. Little by little, you will
sense that it is He who is manifesting himself,
speaking and working through you. You are you,
and at the same time, you are not yourself. You
wanted to disappear, and not only have you not
disappeared, you have become more alive than
ever. Everything becomes clearer, everything
improves; true life begins to flow within you,
bringing abundance, splendour and freedom.

24 June

The feast of St John the Baptist takes place on the 24th of June under the guardianship of the Archangel Uriel, who presides over summer. The Church mentions three Archangels: Gabriel, Raphael and Mikhael, who preside over the three great feasts of the winter solstice and the spring and autumn equinoxes. But why is Uriel never mentioned? Uriel is an Archangel of light, and his name means 'God is my light'.

On the feast of St John, which occurs just as the sun enters Cancer, it is customary to light bonfires in the countryside, for this is the celebration of fire, of the warmth that ripens the fruit and all things. In summer, everything is on fire. This is also the fire of love, of physical, sensual love, of this formidable energy that simmers in the veins of all creatures. The feast of St John thus serves to remind disciples that it is essential to learn to work with the fire of divine love in order to transform all their instincts.

25 *June*

*E*very human being possesses a soul and a spirit, and they too have certain needs. Many people do not feel these needs because they have stifled them by indulging in a life without ideals. But these needs are there, and sometimes they manifest in people who are unable to understand their language. Do you believe that the young people who use drugs (and even the adults who tear their hair out over the situation) understand that their attraction to drugs is in reality an expression, a cry from their soul, which is starved for infinity and begging for food?

What is left for the soul in a society where all belief in a divine world has been destroyed, and where economic and social success is held up as an ideal? Since the soul is deprived of the spiritual food it needs to soar into space, it goes searching for it in the material realm, in substances such as alcohol, tobacco and drugs. Yes, when the soul is not given the spiritual food it needs, it tries to make do with material foods, and this is disastrous.

*F*amily is not an end, a goal, but a point of departure. Those who focus all their attention and efforts only on their family, neglecting everybody else around them, do not realize they are creating conditions that foster misunderstandings and hostility on the part of all other families, and this will end up resembling a clash between clans, between tribes.

Worst of all, there is no guarantee that with this mindset, they will even make their own family happy. The proof of this is that today we see more and more families falling apart: after a while, the parents separate and form ties elsewhere, and the children are left with a father on one side and a mother on the other. Is this what we call a happy family life? There are so many notions that need to be straightened out today!

27 June

So many disciples proclaim to others that their Master speaks to them inwardly. Of course, they can say what they like, but there are irrefutable criteria for recognizing whether it really is their Master who speaks to them or if it is simply an illusion stemming from their own wild imaginings. Before claiming that your Master speaks to you, understand that there are three criteria to be met.

First, you are able to distinguish the path to follow clearly, and you are walking resolutely on this path. Next, you are becoming increasingly open to others, capable of understanding, loving and helping all creatures, and you feel an unmistakeable dilation in your heart, which moves you to give constant thanks to the Lord. Finally, your will is freed, and you are able to accomplish unimpeded all that is right, good and beautiful. If you truly fulfil these three conditions, you may hope that the voice you hear is in fact really that of your Master. But is it necessary to go around telling everyone?

28 June

*E*very fault we commit in our thoughts, feelings or actions drives away certain spiritual entities within us who cannot stand this disharmony. Only inferior spirits can tolerate it – the spirits of light leave us. Lead a chaotic life for eight days and you will see that all of heaven's workers have abandoned you, and that you cannot regain the peace, buoyancy and inspiration you once knew.

Your entire future depends on your understanding of this truth: it is by your attitude that you attract or repel the spirits of light. And it is entirely up to you whether the most highly evolved spirits come to dwell in your heart and in your soul. When they do so, you will become master of yourself, steadfast in all circumstances, and you will come to possess your true human face. Your light will shine out into the cosmos, even to the farthest stars, communicating the subtlest vibrations to the plants and the constellations. Accept this truth and you will possess the powerful key to realization.

29 June

*D*o not rebel against your parents or your family, and do not be in a hurry to leave them in the belief that you will be better off elsewhere. If destiny decreed that you should incarnate in this family rather than in another, it is for a reason: you have something to learn from it, something to understand.

There is justice in the universe, an absolute intelligence, which has determined, according to your merits, precisely in what conditions you are to incarnate: in what era, what country, what family and so forth. It is pointless to complain, as it will not change anything. You must accept the situation and work in order to deserve better life conditions in your next incarnation.

30 June

Consider the example of a great artist, a genuine clairvoyant, or a mathematical genius: each of them possesses a gift. And what is a gift? It is an entity that lives in human beings and manifests itself through them. Of course, our contemporaries will never admit that talents and capabilities are entities that inhabit human beings. But how do they explain why people sometimes lose a talent they once had? It is precisely because this talent was a guest who wanted to take up residence in them, but as they created unpleasant conditions by giving over to the disorder born of their passions, their guest eventually left. This has happened to a great many people who, instead of preciously guarding the treasure entrusted to them, squandered it in a life of folly and intrigue. They assumed their talent was theirs to keep forever. No, unfortunately not.

If you do not want to lose your gifts, if you want to enhance them or acquire others, you must prepare a suitable dwelling for these celestial entities: one of peace, harmony and silence. Only then will they come and make their home in you.

1 July

When you feel an inner discomfort, do not let it linger without doing something about it. Stop and take stock of the state you are in – what exactly are you feeling, what has caused it? Try to remember what you have seen and heard, or what you yourself have done, said or thought.

Because something has caused it, and it is good to figure out what, in order to learn a lesson for the future. If you do not find the cause, do not just sit and do nothing. Concentrate and try to dispel this discomfort by connecting with the world of light, which is our only salvation. Immerse yourself in the light, imagine that you are swimming in this purifying and invigorating fluid, and soon you will feel free, a weight will be lifted, and you will be able to continue your work.

2 July

The organs of our body are tuned to work together in harmony for the good of our whole being. That is why all manner of troubles ensue when a foreign element that does not obey this law of harmony is introduced into our body. Who does not know this? So then, why do we not understand that the same thing occurs in the psychic realm?

When, through our thoughts, feelings or desires, we introduce harmful, discordant elements that are contrary to the harmony of our whole inner being, they produce all sorts of discomforts. That is why, when you are feeling troubled and tormented, do not try to find complicated reasons to justify your state, just understand that you have allowed foreign elements (chaotic and sombre thoughts and feelings) to enter your head and heart, and try to get rid of them.

3 July

As long as human beings are not sufficiently evolved to understand the basic truths of the spiritual life, they will need the tangible, material aspects of religion. But the day they finally manage to become more fully developed and awaken within themselves certain subtle centres – known in Hindu philosophy as chakras – they will gain a higher level of understanding of things and will begin to abandon the outer forms, for these forms will no longer seem as vital, intense and powerful as those they are experiencing inwardly. Then they will no longer even need temples and churches.

There are many temples in the world, all of which have their reason for being. Thanks to the fervour of all the faithful who for centuries have prayed within their walls, churches and temples are imbued with a sacred atmosphere. But not even the most beautiful basilica or the most splendid cathedral can compare with a human body that has been purified and hallowed until it has become a true temple. When human beings have made temples of their bodies, and they pray in these temples, the Lord hears and grants their prayers.

4 July

The moment someone causes you the slightest offense, your lower nature* says, 'Teach him a lesson, bite him, hit back!' Whereas your higher nature says, 'Don't let it bother you, old chap, that's how it is, so instead of brooding and trying to get revenge, try to use and transform this vexation. You are an alchemist – you will turn it into gold.' If you listen to this voice, you will embark on a wonderful work of transformation and you will grow.

The higher nature says more: 'Why do you cry for hours on end when you are given the opportunity to get to work? You must even thank heaven that this person was sent to present you with the opportunity to surpass yourself. And you sit there complaining? How stupid you are!' True disciples ignore the advice given by their lower nature, which supports their weakness and sentimentality: they follow the advice of their higher nature, for they wish to become strong.

* See plate and note on p. 396 and 397.

5 July

*P*eople are free only when they succeed in vibrating in harmony with the cosmic Spirit. Only the cosmic Spirit, the Lord, is free, absolutely free, and so it is only in so far as they become one with the Lord that people will become truly free themselves, because the freedom of the Lord will enter them. If they draw away from the Lord or cut themselves off from Him, that's it, they will no longer be free. They may think that they are free, but the truth is that they are slaves to other forces, other wills, other influences that are guiding them without them realizing it.

So we should beg the Lord not to leave us free, but to take us into His service, for God's freedom infuses the hearts of those who wish to serve Him. In this way, almost without knowing it, we are driven to accomplish only enlightened, fair and noble acts, because we are inspired by others – by divine entities.

6 July

If you are always waiting to be loved, you will never be happy because you are depending on things, which are uncertain. One moment you will be loved, but the next moment anything could happen. Never count on the love of others. This love may come, of course, it may even keep on coming, and if it does, so much the better, but it is wiser not to count on it.

That is why I say to you, 'Do you want to be happy? Then do not ask to be loved, just continue loving; love others day and night and you will always be happy.' Perhaps one day you will be given an extraordinary love… Yes, why not? It could happen, but do not expect it. This is how a wise man solves the problem: he relies on his own love, he wants to love and, if others do not want to love, that is their business. They will be unhappy, but he is happy.

7 July

You must pay attention to your thoughts, for they are living entities. Some are like children who need to be fed, washed and educated: without your realizing, they cling to you, sap your strength and wear you out. Others go out into the world to steal, ransack and plunder, but as there is a spiritual 'police', they come to find you and accuse you for the havoc your children have caused. When you are brought before the invisible courts and you are made to pay damages with interest, you will know suffering, sorrow and remorse.

So, from now on, you must work on your thoughts and desires in order to produce angelic, divine children who will surround you and bring you blessings.

8 July

It is written in the Psalms, *'I walk before the Lord in the land of the living.'* This land of the living is a state of consciousness. In a way, it is also our earth, but on the etheric plane, for the earth is not only the part that we perceive – it is also a subtle world inhabited by luminous beings, angels and divinities.

Jesus is found on this earth too. Jesus has not left the earth, because he said, *'I am with you until the end of the age'*. Of course, he left the physical earth, but he lives on the etheric, living, light-filled, divine earth. When people, here on our earth, manage to purify themselves, and raise themselves spiritually, they too begin to inhabit this land of the living and to communicate with the great Masters, the angels, the divinities and the Christ.

9 July

*A*ll human beings possess in seed form spiritual bodies (the causal, buddhic and atmic bodies)* which one day will develop fully. Each of you will almost certainly have sensed this at some time. You hear some music, or you see a face, and you tremble, you are impelled to work for the good of the whole world; this is a manifestation of the buddhic body, which is beginning to vibrate within you. Or else, you feel a spiritual force flowing through you, powerful enough to move heaven and earth. This is the atmic body trying to make its way through. Or perhaps you receive illumination and the order of the universe is revealed to you, you understand its laws and how it functions; this is the causal body creating a space for itself in your brain.

If these manifestations happen frequently, this means that the three bodies – causal, buddhic and atmic – are already beginning to take possession of your whole being.

* See plate and note on p. 396 and 397.

10 July

You wish to meditate but you do not know how to control your thoughts. Let us suppose that you want to stop a galloping horse. If you stand in front of it, you will be trampled on, so you must run alongside it holding the bridle or the mane, and rein it in. The same goes for your thoughts. If you try to stop them suddenly while they are in full flight in order to concentrate on a specific subject, they will not stop; and if you are too insistent, your brain will seize up.

In order to concentrate, you must first tame the runaway horse that is within you, and to do this you should not oppose it, or your nervous system will be the one to receive a shock. Let your horse run freely for a moment, and when you feel that it has jumped around enough and is no longer on guard, hop onto its back and ride it in the direction you have chosen.

11 July

So many people in society are intelligent, enterprising, and determined! But these qualities they were given for the glory of God and the good of the whole world are being used for their own interests. By doing this, they are severing their link with God.

Obviously, in the short term, cutting this link does not deprive them of their faculties; they have several full boxes, crates and instruments in reserve. This does not all disappear in one fell swoop, any more than a beam disintegrates immediately when woodworm begins to eat at it. They will no longer receive any supplies, they will no longer receive any fresh water, but as they still have some stock, they can continue to live on it and get good results. But this cannot go on forever; given that their supplies are no longer replenished, fermentation, rot, germs and worms begin to destroy them, and one day they will collapse, suffer privation, or become ill because they have stopped drawing from the Source.

12 July

Nature created the two poles – masculine and feminine – which are represented by men and women, so that they might create by making exchanges. These exchanges occur not only on the physical plane, but also on the spiritual plane through words, thoughts or glances, and they are just as vital as nutrition or breathing. If human beings knew how to make these exchanges, they would always be happy and well, but as many do not, they poison themselves. Whereas others, who stop making exchanges, die psychically or spiritually.

We must make exchanges, but exactly as we do with the sun. The sun is high up there in the sky, and the exchanges with it take place on a subtle level, through its warmth and its light. If you were to embrace the sun (supposing such a thing were possible!), you would be burned; so you must embrace it simply by looking at it and thinking of it. If in our desire to love men or women we were content merely to embrace them from afar, we would experience another subtle and poetic life.

13 July

*A*ll religions speak of a potion for immortality, which the alchemists have called the elixir of immortal life. It is true that this elixir can be found on the physical plane, but not just anywhere; it is found only in the most subtle and pure regions. If some initiates recommend going to the sunrise, it is because this is the most favourable time of day to drink this ambrosia, which the sun distributes everywhere and whose particles are received by the whole of creation – by rocks, plants, animals and humans alike.

You must all feed your physical bodies; this is necessary, but it is not enough. You must learn to nourish your subtle bodies, and the food of the subtle bodies is light.

14 July

We speak of angelic hierarchies because there are differences of degree or level among them. Angels are the closest to human beings, and are much superior to them, although they are much lower on the hierarchical ladder than the cherubim and the seraphim. The cherubim and seraphim are so exalted that they are not even aware of the existence of the inhabitants of the earth, and are never given the task of watching over them; they take care of the solar systems and the galaxies, and it is exceedingly rare for one of them to come and meet us.

A seraph moves through space at the speed of lightning. If you are there, alert, ready to grasp something of its celestial radiations, you will have such a dazzling, illuminating experience that the effects will be with you for the rest of your life. But you will not stop the seraph, who will continue its journey through infinite space.

15 July

Instead of studying the methods of our Teaching and putting them into practice, many people prefer to read occult books which they can neither understand nor make use of. They are all just theories – theories that are often inaccurate and even contradictory – and people simply cannot make sense of them. It is time they understood that the only thing that really matters is life, the divine life they should be living, for it is this alone which will give them all the knowledge of heaven and earth. Those who are content merely reading books are wasting their time; and even if they are quite capable of telling you all about what they have read, one senses that behind their eloquence lies emptiness, for no love or light emanates from them.

Knowledge is almost useless if it is not enlivened by love and light. If after your studies and your readings you are still unable to be more fraternal and warm-hearted, then you have understood nothing of true initiatic science.

16 July

Materialists have very little power on the plane of thoughts and feelings because they identify too much with the physical, material world. They have no faith in the possibilities offered by the inner world, and even go so far as to try and erase all trace of this world.

Obviously, the danger for those leading a spiritual life is that once they realize they have the power to change the train of their thoughts and feelings, transforming their sorrow into joy, and their discouragement into hope, they imagine they can just as easily change the outside world. Well no. Through our psychic faculties, we can get in touch with the spiritual world and live in light, love and joy. Although this world is a reality, it is not a concrete, material reality. The objective world and the subjective world both exist and rather than confuse the two, we should recognize the correspondences between them so that we can adjust them.

17 July

There are too many singers who, through their voices, transmit unhealthy, discordant vibrations to their audience, thus causing them to regress towards chaotic, troubled and passionate states. Where are those whose voices inspire in their audience the desire to abandon their dull and mediocre lives for a new life, devoted to beauty and light?

If you want to sing, try to be aware of the role you are about to play in awakening the souls of the whole world and learn to work on your vocal cords by means of your thoughts. Here is an exercise you can do: imagine that you are bathed in a radiant light as you sing before a huge crowd, and bear in mind that through your voice will come powerful, subtle energies, which will enter and electrify the souls of everyone in your audience. Their hearts will open, their minds will be enlightened, and they will decide that in future they will work for the good of the world. If you practise this for months and even years, the day will come when your voice will awaken the higher, divine nature in others.

18 July

When I say that we should unite and become a single collective being, you must understand me. Physically we will always remain separate individuals, with a body, a name and an identity; it is inwardly that we must learn to live the collective life, the cosmic life, the universal life. Sometimes, two people are so much in love that they feel they are one. But they still have two different bodies, which can never be merged into one. Even when they embrace, no matter how much they love each other, they are still two people, and if they get on a bus, or go to the theatre, they will still need two tickets and two seats. Only in their thoughts can they become one and in this same way, all human beings can also become one. Moreover, this sense of unity is independent of physical distance. We can be separated by thousands of miles and still feel united and linked together.

So let us work to introduce this idea of unity into our thoughts, feelings and actions, and then, whilst still remaining separate individuals, we will form one single family, the Universal White Brotherhood everywhere on earth.

19 July

Instead of complaining about external conditions, you must find ways to become stronger, yourselves; otherwise, the slightest things in life become unbearable. Light is the most marvellous thing in nature, but if your eyes are a bit irritated, light will hurt them. If your stomach or your liver is upset, even the finest food will seem indigestible. Someone gives you a warm handshake or an affectionate pat on the back, but if you are crippled with rheumatism, you will cry out in pain. In the same way, even a visit from your dearest friends can plunge you into grief, for if your heart, soul or body is sick, even the best and most beautiful things will be a source of pain for you.

Whereas if you are in good health, a crust of bread, a blow, or even a harsh word will seem delightful, and you will overcome your difficulties without even noticing them.

20 July

Science concentrates on the objective world, because it is solid and stable, and is perceived by everyone in the same way; but it leaves aside the subjective world, because it is changeable and subtle, and therefore less easy to grasp, measure or classify.

Of course, in order to study the psychic life and chart the movements of the soul and the spirit, we would need instruments that we are not yet able to build, but this is not a reason for denying the possibility of such study. Scientists are compromising themselves with such an attitude. It would be wiser if they said, 'This field could hold prodigious riches, it may even be the true science, but we lack the necessary devices to explore it given the current state of our capabilities and means of investigation. We will try to do so in the future, but for the moment we are limiting ourselves to studying what is accessible to our five senses.' That is what they should say if they were really honest and wise.

21 July

*H*ow many men and women are aware that they could do work with their love? To them, love is simply for their own pleasure, and that is why the energies of love turn into poison in the long run. We must understand the importance of this question, and think about devoting our energies to God, by saying, 'Here Lord, I consecrate this love that I feel bubbling up inside me to your glory and to the coming of your Kingdom.'

Obviously, this way of looking at things surprises you – you did not think that you could dedicate your love to heaven; you believed that your feelings and sensations concern only you, and have nothing to do with heaven. That may be so, but if they do not involve heaven, then it is hell that will get involved. For, in this realm, when you say 'my love concerns only me' this 'me' who is only interested in the selfish enjoyment of pleasure is already a part of hell! Why do people exclude heaven from their love as though they felt that what they were doing were shameful (in which case why are they doing it?), as if they had to hide from it? Be careful, if they are not ashamed when it comes to hell, well then hell will come and feast on them.

22 July

In order to transform themselves, disciples must do a great inner work – no true transformation can be brought about mechanically from the outside. Hindus say, 'When the disciple is ready, the Master appears.' This saying is very profound; it clearly indicates that it is always the disciple who must begin the work. When the necessary efforts have been made, it is certain that help will come. A universal law of love and mutual aid exists which can be activated only if you yourself begin the work.

So stop counting on the miracles your Master should do for you, and you will advance rapidly, for he can then be of much greater help to you. Does this seem mysterious to you? Well no, there is nothing mysterious about it: when you are always fixated on someone, and expect him to do everything for you, you paralyze him and he can do nothing for you. So, work, prepare yourself, and the moment you are ready, you will receive the help you need.

23 July

*O*ver hundreds and even thousands of years, instincts have had plenty of time to develop and to become entrenched in human beings. Whereas intelligence, reasoning and wisdom, which appeared in them much more recently, are still very fragile. In reality, intelligence and wisdom existed long before all these other manifestations, but as they belong to regions far removed from human beings, they have a long way to travel before they can manifest in them, and indeed, they are not always welcomed.

Wisdom predates the creation of the world. It is written in the Book of Proverbs, *'The Lord created me, wisdom, at the beginning of his work, the first of his acts of long ago. Ages ago I was set up, at the first, before the beginning of the earth… When he marked out the foundations of the earth, then I was beside him, like a master worker, and I was daily his delight.'* So, wisdom appeared first, but it only settled itself in human beings a short time ago, and that is why, while instinct is solidly entrenched and resistant, wisdom is still very fragile.

24 July

*H*umans know everything but they do nothing. They know that with patience, there is a better chance of achieving lasting results, but they are not patient. They know that gentleness can work wonders, but they always get angry. They know, they know – but they remain weak, vulnerable, lacklustre, sickly and unhappy.

In the Teaching of the Universal White Brotherhood, disciples learn that knowledge is of value only if it is applied in life. It is work that counts, the work of the will, manifesting your knowledge through your behaviour. In ordinary schools, only your academic knowledge is taken into account. That you may one day become a criminal is of no importance – you delivered a good speech, so here is your diploma! The Initiates, on the other hand, do not look at how you expound your knowledge, but how you apply it; if they find your application to be lacking, they will not grant you a diploma. In some cases, they may not even accept you into their school.

25 July

*L*earn to speak with the spirits of nature so as to encourage them to work for the good of humanity. For example, if you are by the sea, speak to its inhabitants, 'Spirits of the waters, unite, and with each ship that passes, inspire in those aboard the wish to improve themselves, to change something in their lives.' Obviously, humans are tough and not easily influenced, but it does not matter.

All those invisible creatures whom you have alerted are already on the move. You have set them to work, and they like to be kept busy. Most of them do not know what it means to work for a divine idea, because the spirits of nature have no moral sense; they have no concept of good and evil, and they are only afraid of a cosmic force that they do not know very well. As they have no moral sense, they can be used either for good or evil purposes. This is why, when some occultists wish to use them in their exercise of black magic, they calmly obey. So why don't you, at least, use them only for good, for the realization of the kingdom of God?

26 July

*I*f people knew how to study the smallest acts of their daily life with a view to interpreting them, just by getting dressed and undressed each day, they would understand that they are repeating the process of incarnation, the descent into matter, and disincarnation, the return to the spirit. Just as when we get dressed, we begin by putting on the lightest clothes (undershirt, shirt and so on) and finish with the heavy overcoat, it is the same when we incarnate on the earth: we enter bodies of increasing density until we reach the physical body.

If human beings have not yet learned to recognize themselves as they truly are, it is because they are still wrapped in several layers. To know themselves, they must divest themselves of all these clothes; in other words, they must break free from their physical, astral and mental bodies, in order to live solely in their divine bodies – that is, the causal, buddhic and atmic bodies.*

* See plate and note on p. 396 and 397.

27 July

*I*f we do not know how to draw the line, even the best things can become harmful. Unfortunately, moderation is not the most common of virtues among human beings. For example, instead of taking only as much joy or pleasure as they need to be stimulated, people gorge themselves until they fall sick. They are like the man whose friend had invited him to dinner: 'Let me see', he said, 'Monday I'm having dinner with so-and-so, so Tuesday I'll be in bed. Wednesday, I'm dining with someone else, so Thursday I'll also be in bed. Well, I can make it Friday, if you like!' At least he knew himself!

Whether it is food, drink or pleasure, human beings always tend to go over the limit. Why can't they be satisfied with just a little? Even poison can be beneficial if it is taken in homoeopathic doses. But except for medicines, human beings do not understand what homoeopathy is – they do not realize that there are homoeopathic doses and allopathic doses in the psychic life too, and that homoeopathic doses are preferable, whereas allopathic doses that are too strong are sometimes harmful.

28 July

*M*ost people wait for their vacation to rest, but they actually return from their holidays completely drained, because they spent all their physical and psychic energies lazing around, or else in useless or demeaning occupations. In order to make good use of their holidays, they should devote them to spiritual work. When we have spent several months of the year in tiring work and all sorts of other obligations, the best form of rest is spiritual work: praying, meditating, purifying oneself, living in peace, admiring the hand of the Creator in nature, and filling one's mind with divine matters.

Do not believe that I am narrow-minded and fanatical to the point of wishing to deprive people of all life's pleasures. On the contrary, I wish to show them the way, to engage them on the path to even greater pleasures. The true spiritual life is so rich in pleasures and joys that there are too many to list. Yet, most people deprive themselves of all this, preferring instead a few physical pleasures, on the pretext that they are on holiday and need to have fun.

29 July

When you climb to the Rock of Prayer in the morning, to watch the sunrise, do you ever think to send it your love and your good thoughts? You should love this Rock! You should even touch and caress it; then its vibrations will change towards you and you will experience great joy. Yes, caress it from time to time as if you were caressing the hand of your beloved. Of course, it is rather rough like the hide of an elephant, but that does not matter; like the elephant, it is full of goodness. Do not let appearances fool you. You believe that the Rock is dead and without a soul… Well no, an extraordinary story has been unfolding around it for millions of years, and it is capable of telling you about it. If you know how to listen to it, it will teach you.

The time is coming when you will need to know how to communicate with all of nature, to feel that everything is alive, that you can speak to rocks, flowers and animals, to water, air, light, and even to the stars, and that they in turn can teach you.

30 July

*E*verything in nature is there to teach us and to make us think. Consider a fruit, a peach, for example. It is made up of skin, flesh and a stone. The skin is the protective layer, which corresponds to the physical plane; the flesh that we eat and that contains life corresponds to the psychic plane (the soul); finally, the stone that we plant in order to grow other trees corresponds to the divine plane (the spirit).

These three parts of the fruit also correspond to the three fundamental virtues of wisdom, love and truth. The fruit's skin represents wisdom: it protects, envelops and preserves it. The flesh of the fruit is the love that is offered to feed all creatures. Lastly, the stone represents truth. We plant the stone so that it can give birth to a new tree, and only what is true can perpetuate life.

31 July

Why do you have this particular bad habit, or that particular physical or psychic disability? Because in your past lives, you were ignorant and let yourselves lead unreasonable lives. All these mistakes have accumulated, condensed and solidified as tumours, and now you find yourselves faced with resistant matter. So, what can you do? Reverse the process by melting these tumours in the fire of the spirit, and creating other forms and expressions that are purer and more harmonious.

In order to transform ourselves, in order to reshape our temperament, our tendencies, our habits, and even our heredity, we must attract divine fire. We must call on it, plead with it to come down, and then ceaselessly blow on it, fan it, so that it can melt us; then, by means of thought, we must work tirelessly in order to create new forms within ourselves.

1 August

When the night is clear, make a habit of looking up at the stars and drinking in this peace that softly descends from the star-studded sky. Link yourself with each of them, and just like a living, intelligent soul, each star will say a word to you. Try to find one with which you feel a special affinity, link yourself with it, and imagine that you are going toward it or that it is coming to speak to you.

The stars are highly advanced souls. By listening to their voice, you will find the solution to many problems, you will feel enlightened and at peace.

2 August

You take an apple, cut it into pieces and eat it: this gives you a particular sensation. If you bite straight into the apple, you have a different sensation. Now, go up to an apple tree, pull a branch towards you and start biting into an apple without picking it – you have yet another sensation. You can feel how alive this apple is, and you experience a sense of well-being, an exquisite taste, and a joy that the tree itself imparts to you because it is connected to the earth and draws forces from the earth, which you then draw towards yourself. By means of its fruit, the tree has served to put you in contact with the earth.

This example can be transposed to the domain of love. Suppose that a man or a woman has cut their ties with heaven – they are like a fruit detached from the tree: they have already lost part of their energies and of their magnetism, so what will you then be able to 'taste'? You will of course find a few crumbs to nibble on, you will have some sensations, but you will not feel that you are linked to the immensity of this source of divine love. Whereas if you love someone who is connected to the Tree of Life, you will feel like you are in communion with the centre of the universe, with the cosmic ocean.

3 *August*

*T*he light is always fearsome to those who live in darkness. This is why the élite, the great Masters, who work for the evolution of humanity are often persecuted. Since the two principles of good and evil constantly battle in the world, those who work for the light necessarily awaken the forces of darkness. The Initiates who wish to improve the world inevitably touch the personal, selfish or shady interests of individuals who then retaliate with all the means at their disposal.

When great spiritual Masters come down to earth to help human beings, they know beforehand that they will be met with all kinds of hostile manifestations: hatred, slander and persecution intended to prevent the work that it is their mission to accomplish. But they never let themselves become discouraged; they continue to work and pour all their love on human beings even if the latter are unconscious and ungrateful.

4 August

*I*t is very important to know how to be active and dynamic by means of thought. In a horoscope, this quality is indicated when Mars and Mercury are in conjunction or well aspected. However, Jupiter, as well as Venus and the Sun must also be involved, otherwise there will be power, but it will not be beneficial in nature. Mars and Mercury provide capacity, strength, dynamism and ardour, but they do not necessarily push in the right direction. They are intellectual forces, forces of willpower that can be used for good or for evil. But if Jupiter, Venus and the Sun also have their say, all this activity is oriented in the best direction: devotion to collective life, to light and divine glory.

5 August

Cosmic Intelligence teaches us a great lesson through the metamorphosis of a caterpillar into a butterfly. For a certain period of their existence (which may last for millions of years), human beings are like caterpillars that need to eat leaves, which means they satisfy their appetites at the expense of others, whom they sully and tear apart. But the day they are disgusted with themselves and decide to become something better, they begin to concentrate, to meditate and above all, to prepare a cocoon to protect themselves; and this cocoon is the aura.

When disciples become aware of the aura's power, and understand that by working on it, they can transform themselves into a butterfly – that is to say, into an initiate – they no longer 'eat' people, just as a butterfly no longer eats leaves, but feeds on the nectar of flowers. Whether you are an ordinary person or an initiate depends on how you feed yourself.

6 August

Jacob's ladder is the symbol of the angelic hierarchy that links human beings and God, and which in the Cabbalah, is represented by the Tree of Life, the Sephirotic Tree.* To imagine as some people do that we can speak directly to God simply demonstrates great ignorance.

On earth, it is impossible to meet with an important person unless we go through intermediaries and yet, where the Lord is concerned, we can go right up to him without the slightest problem! For the Lord, you see, is a kindly gent who is very accessible, whose beard we can pull and whose shoulder we can slap! In reality, if there were no transformers, that is, these hierarchies that form the link between humans and God, there would not be the least trace left of anyone who approached the Lord: they would be struck down.

* See the note and figure on pp. 398-401.

7 August

We see many people attach themselves to creatures who cut them off from heaven, who prevent them from uniting with the sublime world, from praying, meditating, studying and even from just being good. These people stupidly allow themselves to be influenced without even perceiving the abyss into which they are about to plunge. Yes, no judgment at all, no criteria!

I am not against associations, friendships, love and marriage. But to go and forge ties with someone who does not help you get closer to the Lord, who does not enlighten you, purify you, or ennoble you... To forget the source of love from which we can drink day and night, only to go and draw from tiny swamps and puddles, hoping to be fulfilled, to be filled with wonder – well, that makes no sense!

8 *August*

Some people wait for life to teach them about themselves, and indeed, life is well equipped to teach them, but it takes a lot of time and it is very costly. They must know that there is another more economical way, which is to ask heaven to place them in front of a true mirror, that is, before a great being who has no interest in deceiving them or taking advantage of them. Where can we find such a mirror? In an Initiate. This is who you must ask, 'What is inside me? Which weaknesses must I tackle, which talents must I develop? For what type of work am I predestined?' And as he is disinterested, he will give you impeccable answers.

Now, if this mirror were to start reflecting a few of your flaws, should you be furious with it? On the contrary, you should thank heaven and say, 'Now that I know myself, I will avoid so many disasters, and I will spare others and myself many misfortunes!'

9 August

In order to fulfil their educational role properly, families must not be afraid to abandon certain ideas that have a harmful influence on the harmony of society. For, it is such ideas that teach children to desire their own personal success and their own wellbeing above all else, even if it is at the expense of others.

Families also accustom their children to regard those who are not of the same nationality, religion or race as inferiors or enemies. Therefore, it should come as no surprise if these children later grow up to become selfish, narrow-minded and intolerant adults.

10 August

*E*very day, think about introducing harmony within you; absorb it and breathe it in. Once it has penetrated every part of your being and tuned you like an instrument, the divine spirit itself will come and play you.

Harmony is the result of the union between mind and heart, soul and spirit. The moment your soul melds with the Cosmic Spirit, you experience ecstasy. For this is what ecstasy is: a bolt of lightning that occurs when the human soul unites with the divine spirit. All your impurities are burned away in this intense fire, this blaze, and finally, you are unburdened, free to fly in space and you melt into universal harmony.

11 August

*T*he most essential, most glorious work that heaven asks of us is to participate in the realization of God's kingdom. When you come to the fraternal meetings, instead of being scattered and allowing your thoughts to wander all over the place, always bring them back in this direction: the kingdom of God and his righteousness. As there are many of us and we congregate often, the forces and energies that we emanate accumulate in divine reservoirs, and one day, they will give results. When? That is not our concern.

We meet together to bring about the kingdom of God, and even supposing that our thoughts and desires do not succeed in making it happen, it will come to dwell within us. It will be given to us because we will have worked for it. If other people do not wish to accept it, it will be sent back to us. We have nothing to lose by working for a sublime ideal.

12 August

When the sun rises on the horizon, which places see it first: the abysses, the precipices or the high mountain peaks? Of course, you will say it is the peaks. So then why aren't you able to interpret this phenomenon? Why is it that in life, you think initiates are mistaken and the masses are right in their judgements? How is it that the Lord would reveal himself to all sorts of people who have no conscience or morals yet deprive the initiates – who live in purity and demonstrate the greatest abnegation – of his light? How can you fail to see the lack of logic in your reasoning?

In reality, the initiates are the first to be enlightened, the first to show that they are in unison with light, the first to discover the sublime truths. As for all those who remain too low down, God alone knows when they will be enlightened!

13 August

A Master always bears in mind the existence of the higher entities to whom he will one day be accountable. If he were to forget these beings and think only of his disciples, he would unwittingly do harm because it is inevitable: if we cut our ties with heaven we can do only wrong. So, the important thing for you is not to know whether or not you matter to your Master, but to observe whether or not you are growing spiritually richer, stronger, wiser, better and happier. If this is the case, then do not concern yourself with the rest.

Rid yourself of the desire to matter to your Master. Simply know that you matter to him insofar as you are part of his work, in that he must instruct you in the true science, lead you on the true path, and give you what he himself has received. What is important to him is your divine self; it is for this that he works. As much as the celestial entities matter to your Master, so too does your divine being. You are therefore no less valuable to him than the celestial entities, but when I say 'you', I am speaking of your soul and your spirit.

14 August

The phoenix is the symbol of highly evolved beings who, knowing the laws of life and immortality, are able to renew themselves continually. These beings have modelled themselves on the sun. This is why anyone who aspires to immortal life must seek out the sun, because only the sun can teach them what elements will give them immortality, and how to work with them.

There are three such elements: light, heat and life, which the sun never ceases to distribute through space. The day you understand this truth and prepare yourself to attend the sunrise as if it were an event surpassing all others, you will then drink the sun, you will nourish yourself with the sun and you will become immortal.

15 August

It happens that when a man sees a woman embracing the spiritual life in order to perfect herself, rather than rejoicing, he tries to stop her. He does not understand that if his wife becomes inwardly rich, he too will benefit. The same is true for a woman who wants to oppose her husband's spiritual evolution.

In reality, we cannot prevent a soul from going towards the light; the soul is the daughter of God, no one has a hold on it. Of course, it is never advisable for a husband or a wife to start neglecting their obligations using spirituality as a pretext. On the contrary, the one who feels the most drawn to the spiritual life must use their intelligence and heart to maintain harmony between them, and so encourage and convince their partner; they must certainly not put the other person off spirituality with a fanatical attitude. It is important for a man and a woman who are in a relationship together to be aware of this. With tenderness, kindness and patience, one can teach the other and lead them towards the Creator.

16 August

Most people think that by devoting their time to their work, their family and their friends, they are doing everything they must. Of course, it is very commendable to be dutiful, diligent and conscientious. But that is not enough, and there is no justification for neglecting the divine world.

Despite their morality and their virtue, those who neglect heaven exclude from their lives everything that can bring them inspiration, beauty and immortality. They must understand that there exists a higher morality, one that teaches that it is not enough to be in agreement with the laws of the earth and of society, because the earth is still far from the perfection of heaven. They must constantly seek to attune themselves with heaven, by fulfilling all their duties towards it.

17 August

Absolute justice exists but this justice must not be sought outside ourselves where it does not exist; there is no justice outside us. Absolute justice, divine justice is above us, because everything is recorded and we cannot escape the consequences of these recordings. Even when you are alone in your room concocting some dubious scheme and you think, 'No one has seen me, no one will convict me', in reality, everything is already recorded inside you.

For nature has placed devices – meters – inside human beings, and these meters register so much water, so much gas, so much electricity, in other words, how many thoughts, how many feelings, how many actions, and of what nature. Everything is recorded. Try, therefore, to do good things even when you are at home on your own, because these good things will be recorded. God is often portrayed as an eye inside a triangle. This is a way of showing that God has installed recording devices in human beings.

18 August

*E*veryone has their own temperament, and according to their nature, they like certain things and detest others – this is perfectly normal. But if they do not call upon the help of a higher element called wisdom, self-mastery or willpower, to control and give direction, it is safe to say that they are headed straight for disaster. Granted, they have these impulses – every one of us is driven by instinctive forces, whether from the stomach, the intestines or the genitals. There is always something pushing us, but that is no reason to let ourselves go.

This is why, whenever you are impelled to do something, ask yourself, 'Alright, what will the result be if I give in to it?' Of course, as long as your consciousness is not awakened, there are still many things that can bring you joy. However, these joys turn into suffering, bitterness and regret, whereas the joys of a wise, enlightened person remain pure gold. We must not deprive ourselves of joy or pleasure, but just be aware of their nature, and replace them with better, purer, nobler and more beneficial joys and pleasures.

19 August

Many people, who have neither wisdom, nor light, nor work methods, imagine that others will consider them to be great authorities, and that they will succeed in everything. But as the opposite happens, they think that they are victims and that the whole world is against them. Well, this is the worst kind of attitude.

Those who realize that they are unsuccessful with others must say to themselves, 'I see that I am not prepared to do my job properly. When I ought to have shown love, sensitivity and caring, I was in fact closed, hard and stubborn. When I should have trodden lightly and had more self-control, I was tactless and impatient'. This is what a disciple does. Instead of blaming the whole world for their failures, they develop humility and accept that they have much to learn. Only then will success and positive results be possible for them.

20 August

*I*t is not enough to understand something; we must apply it. For many people, understanding and application are worlds apart. They understand, they understand, but when it comes to actually accomplishing, they are unable to do so.

In initiatic science, understanding is not separate from realization. If you are unable to manifest what you claim to have understood, then you have not really understood. If you had understood, you would have realized. Yes, for initiates, to know is to have the ability. If you are not able, then you do not know – there are still some gaps in your knowledge, elements you are missing for successful realization.

21 August

*T*hinkers and artists have a duty to reflect on the effects their works may have upon others, because even if human justice leaves them in peace, divine justice will hold them accountable. One day, when they arrive in the other world, they will be shown the damage they have done, and no matter how much they protest, saying that they have not caused all this harm, the reply will be, 'Yes, these people have suffered because of you, you introduced turmoil into their minds and hearts, you drove them to try risky experiences without warning them of the dangers they ran, you are guilty and you will be punished.'

Everyone must take care to use their gifts to enlighten others, awaken in them love, confidence and the desire to better themselves. Otherwise, they must know that not only will they be punished, but in a future incarnation, they will also be deprived of these gifts.

22 August

When you eat, you are careful not to swallow just anything. Well, you must be equally careful that the thoughts and feelings you absorb and digest are pure.

Customs officers are placed at the border of every country to check what comes in and what goes out. Have you also placed customs officers at the borders of your own country to make sure that nothing dangerous or harmful is allowed to pass through? No, you have not, so anything from anywhere gets in and you are poisoned. Put customs agents in place, and for every thought and feeling that arises, immediately say, 'Wait a second, where do you come from? What will you bring me if I let you in?' This way, you will anticipate the consequences of a thought or a feeling that comes to visit you, and chase it away if it does not seem very 'Christian' to you.

23 *August*

Sometimes we see yogis do incredible contortions with their body: they twist their limbs and roll their bellies in every direction, making their veins and arteries pop out. We are amazed by such mastery! But is it truly worthwhile wasting years to obtain such results? They have undoubtedly achieved great mastery of their physical body, but have they done the same work in the spiritual realm? Do they know how to control their feelings and thoughts? Often, they do not even know how to conduct themselves in their inner lives.

Of course, the physical body is important, for we could do nothing on earth without it; but all the physical body needs is for us to be vegetarian, do some simple gymnastic exercises, and lead a pure and balanced life. What counts most is to study spiritual laws, to apply them and to achieve mastery of our psychic life.

24 August

Like trees, human beings receive energy from the cosmic ocean, and they receive this energy not only through their roots, but also through their leaves and flowers – symbolically speaking.

Through their roots, they penetrate deeply into the soil, but from this soil, they draw only physical energy. A human being's roots are represented by the organs situated below the diaphragm: the stomach, intestines and genitals. The leaves are represented by the lungs and the heart. Finally, the head, with its mouth, ears, nose and eyes, is comparable to the leaves and flowers, which receive far more subtle energies, although not as subtle as the brain, and beyond that, the spirit which captures divine energies. You must therefore awaken the spirit within you and set it in motion, for only the spirit is capable of capturing divine energies.

25 *August*

*I*n the morning, when you go to contemplate the sun, imagine that by drawing nearer to the centre of our universe, you are drawing nearer to your own centre. In getting closer to the sun, you become more alive because the sun is the fire of life.

Every morning, draw near to the sun and tell yourself that you can capture a spark or a flame that you will bury deep inside and carry preciously as if it were the greatest treasure. Thanks to this flame, your life will be purified, sublimated, and everywhere you go, you will bring purity and light.

26 August

*B*ecause human beings have lost touch with the invisible world, they are unaware that through their thoughts and feelings, they can attract spirits of darkness, repulse spirits of light, and vice versa. This is why they are continually assailed by evil forces. Yes, this is a reality: evil entities exist within and around us, and those who do not know how to protect themselves against them by means of the appropriate psychic work, are troubled and may even fall prey to these undesirables.

Whereas someone who knows how to live in a state of peace, harmony, and inner elevation is able to attract magnificent creatures whose presence also manifests in them – the person feels expansive, bathed in light, as if they were embracing the whole of creation. Although they may not realize it themselves, this is thanks to the presence of these heavenly entities.

27 August

How mistaken people are in thinking that silence is like the desert, a void, the absence of any activity or any creation – in a word, nothingness.

In fact, there is silence and then there is silence. Generally speaking, there are two types of silence: the silence of death and the silence of the higher life. It is precisely the latter – the silence of the higher life – that we need to understand, and that we are talking about here. This silence is not inertia, but intense work that is carried out in the midst of perfect harmony. It is neither a void nor an absence, but a fullness comparable to that experienced by beings united by a great love who are living something so profound that they cannot express it with gestures or words. Silence is a quality of the inner life.

28 August

As the ancient astrologers have taught us, the stars predispose but do not determine. Yes, the stars act on human beings, influencing them to go this way or that. When it comes to highly evolved beings, this influence is not strong enough to be determining; but as most people are so weak, it is exactly as if the stars compelled them to go in a certain direction.

Take the example of a pretty girl. She does not say to the boy she meets, 'Come with me and kiss me.' She does not throw herself at him either, but she puts on airs, she strikes poses, and then the boy throws himself at her. You see, even though she said nothing and did nothing, she still influenced him. Why? Because he is weak. Well, the stars are just like pretty girls: they manage to awaken something in you, and if you are weak, you succumb. They inspire a flash of anger in you and you rush out to strike your neighbour. Later, the stars might say, 'But we didn't make him do it!' Yes, but you have already hit your neighbour on the head.

29 August

At the beginning, love is always something very poetic: two people meet, they exchange a few words, and they are in heaven, inspired and creative.

But as soon as this love becomes physical, they lose their sense of wonder. So many people have noticed this! Yes, they have noticed it, but they do the same thing all over again – instead of protecting their love by remaining in the subtle regions for as long as possible, they hurry to experience it in the coarsest of regions. Out of curiosity and greed, they want to descend and explore the field – and even the subterranean! Afterwards, of course, things are no longer the same. They do not love each other as much or hold each other in such admiration, as they have seen each other too often in situations that were not very aesthetic. Why do they not try to live as long as possible in the world of beauty, poetry and light?

30 August

*I*f you speak without thinking, without weighing your words, you are like a person who enjoys tossing lit matches everywhere they go, which naturally starts fires. Even if you apologize afterwards, 'Oh, I did not mean to say that, I am sorry', it is too late; the houses around you are already burning and reduced to ashes. And that is how you help the forces of darkness in their destructive enterprises.

People are never sufficiently conscious of the damage their words can cause. If you were to seek the origin of the misunderstandings, discord and conflict between human beings, you would see that in most cases, it is the spoken word: someone uttered some nonsense without any real purpose in mind, for the pleasure of talking or to appear interesting.

From now on, try to watch what you say. When you have to speak, do so to improve the lives of those who are listening to you, to enlighten their minds, to warm their hearts and especially to direct their will in the service of a sublime ideal.

31 August

*A*lthough it is not always good to tell the truth, it is always good to know it. Knowing the truth never hurts you. When Jesus said, *'Do not throw your pearls before swine'*, the pearls he was talking about were the truths for which humanity is not yet prepared, and if you reveal these truths to them, not only will they not appreciate them, but they will tear you apart.

The truth does not bring misfortune. It brings misfortune only if you reveal it in front of wicked and shadowy people. So, you must not 'throw' it away; treasure it within you, for it will set you free and strengthen you. Every day, you can thus adorn yourself with the gold and pearls of truth, contemplate and touch them, then lock them up in your inner safe deep within you. What misfortune can this bring? This contact with the truth can only strengthen you, and in this way, you become able to help others, to support and uplift them.

1 September

Someone says to me, 'Oh, the Brotherhood is so wonderful! And with all the things you reveal to us – it's marvellous! It's hard to believe that such a place really exists on earth. But (for there is always a but) when I think about going back to work with people who lead such materialistic and disorderly lives, I just wonder what good it does to try and transform my own life. It seems pointless to try and change anything when I have to go back to living like before.' What can I say to that? Objections of this kind prove that this person has not understood the usefulness and effectiveness of our Teaching.

The Teaching gives us the criteria and methods we need to face all life's difficult conditions. Without the Teaching, we would soon be swept away by all the chaotic currents and pulled under, lost. It is precisely because conditions in life are difficult that the Teaching is so valuable.

2 September

You sometimes close yourself off and lose your love and enthusiasm because you have been disappointed or upset. Well, this is not very clever, for it does nothing to change the events that are upsetting you, and with this attitude, you deprive yourself of something precious. So, it is doubly regrettable!

Whatever your difficulties or sorrows may be, there is no justification for giving in to negative states of mind. You will say, 'But, I am in this state because people have deceived and betrayed me, it is not my fault.' Yes, it is your fault – your reasoning is incorrect. No one is forcing you to be in such a state. Even if people have sought to do you harm, you are not obliged to submit passively to their wickedness, and compound your woes by letting your heart dry up. So, you see, this is not sound reasoning. And if you do not straighten things out, if you abandon hope, love and faith, you are dead. Even before you actually die, you are already dead.

3 September

True disciples have learned to ascend and to descend. They know that they cannot always remain on the high peaks, but neither do they linger too long in the dust, noise and commotion of the valleys. They go up and they come down... They go up again and they come back down again...

When we come down we manifest love; when we go up we are seeking wisdom, we wish to study, meditate and pray. It is not good to study without coming down afterwards to help others with your knowledge. You must get used to this dual movement. The ascetics, hermits and recluses who fled to caves or the desert did not always find the best solution to this problem; neither do those who have never ascended to the summits, that is to say, who have never felt the need for a spiritual life.

4 September

*V*anity comes across as good, kind and generous; it goes everywhere so that it may be seen, it is charitable in order to draw attention to itself, it is helpful so as to be appreciated. But there is no doubt that it is often harmful to those who manifest it, for it destroys them.

Pride, on the other hand, is of no use at all, not even to others. Proud individuals are harsh and contemptuous; they do nothing for others yet still expect to be appreciated and respected. They do not go and parade themselves in public, because they are satisfied with the good opinion they have of themselves. They think others should go to the trouble of discovering them. But when they find that people neither respect nor approve of them, and do not recognize their superiority, they shut themselves off and become morose. With vain people, there is still a light – a somewhat hazy light, granted, but at least they are doing something to shine. Proud people are dark and gloomy. They are under the sign of Saturn, whereas vain people are under the sign of Jupiter.

5 September

Suppose you want to help someone, but through ignorance or clumsiness, you end up hurting them instead. As the justice of this world does not perceive your motives, it will condemn you on the basis of your actions. But the justice on high sees your good intentions, and although it may allow human laws to punish you, because that is not their concern, it will reward you richly for your divine and selfless intentions. Conversely, if you are generous and shower gifts on someone but have an ulterior motive – seducing a girl, for instance – you may be well thought of on earth, but on high, heaven will punish you, because the celestial courts judge your motives not your deeds.

Our actions and the motives that inspire them are not subject to the same jurisdiction. Of course, if both your motives and your deeds are divine and beyond reproach, you will be rewarded on both levels; and if you break the law on both levels, both courts will condemn you.

6 September

The most important aspect of every activity you undertake is the idea behind it, the motive that drives you to act, the goal you want to achieve. The activity itself does not matter much; you should not be concerned with whether or not it will win you the appreciation of others, or bring you money. You may not seem to be accomplishing much by following a spiritual teaching, but if you do so with the desire to foster and uphold the idea of universal brotherhood, you keep adding a few elements to your future, your evolution, thereby changing the whole of your destiny. You may not see any results for a long time, but one fine day, blessings will rain down on you from all around, because all your good work has been recorded and you will reap the rewards for it.

Human beings judge you according to your material achievements, but heaven rewards or punishes you on the basis of your motives. So, if you work to uphold the idea of brotherhood, it is to heaven that you must look for your reward.

7 September

*M*ost people confuse happiness with pleasure. They imagine that whatever pleases, attracts or appeals to them will make them happy. But that is where they are wrong.

Pleasure is a brief and enjoyable sensation that leads you to believe that if only you could prolong it indefinitely, you would be happy. Well, no. Why? Because the activities that give you an enjoyable sensation quickly and effortlessly do not for the most part belong to a very elevated plane. They concern only your physical body, perhaps your heart and barely your intellect. However, we cannot be happy when we seek to satisfy our physical body alone, or even our heart and mind, because such satisfactions are incomplete and short-lived. Happiness, unlike pleasure, is not a fleeting sensation; it is something that concerns the whole of our being.

8 September

No one can escape their karma, but there are different ways of paying it. Prayer is a form of payment, for you put gold in your prayers, that is, all the very best of your heart, your soul and your spirit. You repent your sins and promise to make up for them with good deeds. So heaven says, 'Since this person repents and wants to make amends, it means they have understood – let us ease their trials.'

For, what does heaven want? It wants us to improve. It has no desire to crush us – what good would that do? It simply wishes us to become wiser and more conscious, which is why, if we are too hard-headed, it will continue to send us trials. If, however, it sees that we have understood without the need to endure such hardships, it is satisfied. It has no desire to destroy us.

9 September

Some people wonder how one becomes a black magician. Actually, it is very easy. Anyone who gives free rein to their worst instincts, who continually breaks the laws of goodness, justice, and love, who tries to succeed at the expense of others, to oust and destroy them, cannot help but become a black magician. So, it is quite clear.

Many people imagine that in order to become a black magician, one must have a diabolical master who teaches the art of evil spells and incantations. This is sometimes the case, but you do not necessarily need a master to become a black magician. Anybody can become one even without a master, without anything; it is enough to let oneself be guided by one's lower nature. Similarly, if someone thinks only of helping and enlightening others, they are on their way to becoming a white magician even if they have no master to teach them.

10 September

So many people say, 'I want to live my own life.' Yes, but what kind of life? The life of an animal or a divine life? All those who think only of 'living their own life' lead a meaningless existence. The goal of a disciple must be very different, they must say, 'Lord, I am beginning to realize that without you, without your light and your intelligence, I am nothing. I wanted to do as I pleased, but now I am ashamed and disgusted with myself. I am now ready to serve you, to devote my life to you so that I may at last be of some use to the whole world.'

You must repeat this day and night. Even if the Lord blocks his ears because he is tired of listening to you, carry on, for the Twenty-four Elders will hold a meeting and they will issue a decree about you saying, 'Behold, from this day and this hour forward, your destiny will be changed.' And this decree will be proclaimed throughout every region of space; the angels and all heaven's servants will instantly obey it, and you will see your life transformed.

11 September

You meet a magnificent being whom you like and wish to know better. Instead of trying at any cost to get closer to them on the physical plane, learn to listen to the vibrations of their voice, to perceive the light in their eyes, to rejoice in the harmony of their gestures. In this way, you will gradually form a relationship with all that is the most subtle and divine in them, and experience new and indescribable sensations.

In the same way, you will also discover that the men and women you have tended to look down on or ignore because of their unassuming appearance, are actually exceptional beings who have far more to offer you than other people who are seemingly more interesting or attractive.

12 September

*O*n earth we are continually at the mercy of alternations. At one moment, the sky is blue and the sun is shining, but the next, clouds come between us and the sun, and everything becomes cold and dark. This is true on the physical plane, and it is also true on the spiritual plane.

When human beings lived in paradise, everything was easy for them; but when they began to distance themselves from paradise and descend into matter, they encountered cold, darkness, sickness and death. This is how initiatic science explains the conditions in which we are living today. But there is a region in the universe made of etheric, luminous, radiant matter, where it is always spring. On the physical plane, of course, it is impossible to escape the alternation of the seasons or of happy and unhappy events, but by means of thought, you can rise to this region of eternal spring. For it exists, it is a reality. If you manage to ascend to the world of the spirit, nothing will ever come between you and the sun again, and you will always be illuminated, warmed, vivified and filled with wonder!

13 September

*T*hose who work exclusively for themselves and forget about the collectivity become impoverished and forfeit the esteem and friendship of others. By contrast, when people are full of love, kindness and abnegation, others may consider them to be a little foolish at first, so they exploit and take advantage of them but, as time goes by, these others come to realize that they are truly exceptional beings, and in the long run, everyone treats them with love. However, this does not happen overnight, of course.

When you deposit a sum of money in the bank you do not receive the interest right away, you must wait. Exactly the same law applies in the spiritual realm. You work with a great deal of love, patience and trust and to begin with, you have nothing to show for it, but you must not be discouraged. One day, wealth will come to you from all sides in such abundance that you will not be able to escape it even if you try. The entire universe will shower you with extraordinary riches, because you will have brought them upon yourself. This is justice!

14 September

*O*ur intelligence is a reflection of Cosmic Intelligence – a very imperfect one however, for as it passes through our mind and heart, which are constantly prey to the disorder of our passions, Cosmic Intelligence finds itself limited and dimmed. Cosmic Intelligence cannot manifest itself perfectly through someone who has not yet learned to control their instinctive impulses, but the more we purify and perfect ourselves, the more we will be able to understand and capture the light of this Intelligence.

Once disciples understand that their intelligence depends on the state of all the cells in their body, they endeavour to keep them balanced and in harmony by paying attention to the quality of their physical food, but especially to the quality of their psychic food – their sensations, feelings and thoughts. If they neglect these, they will remain impervious to the greatest revelations. There is no way to improve our intelligence other than by improving our way of life. The initiates have always believed this, they have always known this, and they have always worked accordingly.

15 September

*P*eople believe that their opinions are objective, but the truth is that most of the time, these opinions stem from their needs, and often even their basest needs. Take political ideologies for example. To satisfy the people of Ancient Rome, they were promised bread and games. Still, today, in another form, the people must be promised bread and games.

Take also the theories about sexuality. As most men and women are incapable of controlling themselves, specialists have presented theories that actually have no absolute value. These theories apply only to feeble and ignorant human beings who do not know – and do not want to know – that sexual energy could contribute to their spiritual fulfilment if it were mastered instead of being squandered in the pursuit of pleasure. And so on and so forth with everything else. This is why it is so difficult to instruct human beings. They can truly understand and accept these initiatic truths only to the extent that they have succeeded in ridding themselves of their baser needs, otherwise these needs keep them bound to their misguided opinions.

*I*ntuition is true intelligence. It has no need of research and calculations, it understands instantly. It penetrates everything with a single glance, and tells you what it has discovered. Intuition is both a feeling and an understanding. You feel things at the same time as you understand them. In this higher form of intelligence, the first indispensable element is life. And in situations where everyone else hesitates and doubts, those who possess this intelligence, and believe in it, understand immediately.

Once you begin to discover the true nature of reality, with both its objective and subjective aspects, its outer and inner aspects, you will be amazed to discover how simple everything is.

17 September

Nowadays, rites of initiation no longer take place in temples but in life. It is now life that puts us through the trials of the four elements, which are the trials of matter. When man was cast out of paradise for having disobeyed the Lord, he lost his power over matter – symbolically represented by the four elements. In order to regain this power, he must learn to control his physical body (earth), his feelings (water), his thoughts (air), and master his sexual energy (fire).

But is it still of any use to talk to human beings about mastering their sexual energy? Increasingly, all the rules in this area are being flouted; young people and adults think only of stupidly wasting this force, this quintessence, which is a condensation of sacred fire. And in so doing, they allow sickness and death to penetrate them insidiously.

18 September

We so often hear said, 'If God existed, if there were justice in this world, the good would be rewarded and the wicked punished.' As a matter of fact, good people are rewarded and wicked people are punished, just not at once. Why? Because if the laws punished them immediately for their mistakes, human beings would be wiped out, and they would not even have the chance to mend their ways. Whereas if they are given plenty of time as well as a few small inconveniences to force them to reflect, they will have the opportunity to make amends. And those who do good are not rewarded right away either; if they were, they might well become slack and begin to transgress all the laws. So, heaven gives them time to become stronger and more confident, to know themselves better, and to see to what extent they will continue to do good.

So, there are reasons why the divine laws manifest themselves so slowly, but it is absolutely true that good is rewarded with good and that evil... ends very badly.

19 September

So many people complain that they are sick and unhappy, and yet, when you tell them what to do to free themselves from their sorry state, they say that they do not have the time.

Yes, human beings are incredible: when you tell them how to restore balance, peace and happiness, they never have the time! Well, too bad for them. If they cannot find time to pray, meditate and do some exercises, they are going to have to take time to suffer. Those who have no time for the light will spend time in darkness. Those who have no time for health will have time for illness, tossing and turning in their bed. This is a mathematical certainty, an absolute.

20 September

When you distance yourself from the sun, you suffer from the cold and darkness, and your vitality diminishes. When you draw closer to the sun, the light increases, warmth increases, and life increases. So, it is simple – all creatures who have distanced themselves from the spiritual sun, from God, are deprived of light, warmth and life. This is why their thoughts, feelings and deeds then bear the mark of this deprivation. On the other hand, all those who take the path back towards the Godhead receive light, warmth and life, and they accomplish great things.

Unfortunately, we see that more and more newspapers, magazines and especially books are turning human beings away from the Source, and destroying their faith, their morals, and all sense of the sacred, the divine. So, read them if you wish, for the sake of curiosity, but do not let yourselves be swayed. Focus all your attention on other books, especially on the one that most deserves to be read: the book of nature. It will teach you how to draw closer to the spiritual sun so as to receive its light, warmth and life.

21 September

Medicinal herbs need water to release all their healing properties. You boil, soak or steep the herbs in water, which you then drink. You do not eat the plants themselves; it is enough to drink the water in which they have been soaked, for the water is imbued with the plants' healing properties. You must also know how to use the absorptive power of water to influence your psychic life.

When you are extremely tired, take a bath or simply wash your hands knowing that the water will absorb your fatigue – you will feel lighter. Do the same when you feel troubled, sad, or unhappy – the water will wash away your cares and sorrows. On the other hand, at times when you feel especially happy, inspired and exalted, wait a few hours before washing even your hands. Above all, do not take a shower or a bath because water not only has the ability to absorb negative elements, it also absorbs positive, beneficial elements.

22 September

What does someone who loves their family do in times of need? They make the decision to go abroad to earn money. Someone who does not love their family as much will not have the courage to leave. Although it may seem that the former has abandoned their family, it is only to help them: they go abroad to earn money and everyone is happy when they return. Whereas the person who did not want to leave their family condemns both them and himself to continued poverty.

Now let us interpret this. A true father, a true mother will choose to abandon their family for at least a few moments to go and seek fortune abroad, that is to say, in the divine world where they will gather riches. And upon their return, the whole family will benefit. But those who have not understood this keep their thoughts constantly focused on their family. This is what they call love but what can they bring their family with this kind of love? Not very much – a few trifles, a few mouldy crumbs left in the cupboard. True fathers and mothers go abroad, that is to say, as often as possible they devote a few minutes to link themselves with heaven.

23 September

In general, the astral body* awakens around the age of fourteen. The astral body is the seat of emotions, feelings and passions, and as both its negative and positive aspects are equally developed, it manifests itself in teenagers as much by a need to revolt and destroy as by a need to love.

Of course, even very young children manifest likes and dislikes before the age of fourteen, but not as strongly. From the age of fourteen onwards, feelings dominate, feelings motivate and govern their behaviour. If a young boy or girl feels love for someone, it is useless to try to reason with them in the hope of turning them away from the object of their affections. As they are wholly guided by their feelings and determined to give expression to them, they will refuse to listen. Or else, even if they do listen and yield out of fear, obedience or respect for adults, inwardly they will cling to their feelings, for feelings always reign supreme.

* See plate and note on p. 396 and 397.

24 September

Life is such that you can never be sure of anything, either of events or of other people. They will sometimes think of you, but more often than not, they will forget you. So, if you do not establish something stable within yourself, you will be constantly tossed about and disoriented.

Yes, it is time to begin to recognize the nature of things and understand what you have to do in order to be happy. And since you need love to be happy, since you feel that it is love that makes you blossom and receive revelations, and since you want your love to last forever, well then, you must love without waiting to be loved in return. If those you love return your love, so much the better, give thanks to heaven – but do not count on it. This is the only way that you will become all-powerful, independent, and master of the situation.

25 September

Watch a wood fire burning... Fire teaches us to detach ourselves from coarse, material things – our envelopes, our shells.

All the solar energy accumulated within the tree – that is to say the soul of the tree – is released from the form that held it captive, and returns to the celestial regions from which it came. Yes, the soul goes back to its homeland but it needs the help of fire to free itself. It is fire that opens the thousands of doorways through which the soul of the tree escapes. The crackling sounds we hear are the language of liberation. Where a door is more difficult to open, the soul must pound harder and all these explosions are the soul's song of victory as it frees itself.

26 September

Disciples who want to advance spiritually must strive every day to create a divine image of themselves. Of course, they should not think that they are already divinities, nor must they want others to consider them as such, for that would only draw people's derision or hostility. They will say, 'Who does he think he is? He's going mad!' and they would not be altogether wrong.

So, whatever inner work you undertake, you must continue to behave with unassuming simplicity towards others. Imagine that you are wise, luminous and radiant, that you are fulfilling God's will and that you have recovered the perfection you had long ago in the innocence and splendour of paradise – the perfection that will again be yours in the future. But remember that it has not yet happened!

27 September

*H*uman beings have roots throughout the whole universe, for they have worked for billions of years in every region of space to gather the elements with which they have succeeded in forming their physical, etheric, astral and mental bodies, but also the seeds of their causal, buddhic and atmic bodies*.

Thanks to these different bodies, human beings are in contact with all the regions of the universe, and this is how they are able to touch certain powers that are then reflected on the screen of their consciousness. If a person is sufficiently lucid, when they look at this screen, they can sometimes see that they have stirred up swamps with their thoughts, wishes and desires. But if they succeed in touching heaven, their screen will show them images of splendour from which they learn. In this way, they become conscious, as they say, of the reality of things, they realize that there are laws, and they can then decide to become more intelligent, wise, careful and reasonable, so as to no longer project the same disorder and ugliness onto their screen. Consciousness, therefore, is a stage on which certain actors appear to portray something of their dark, selfish lower nature, or of their luminous, vast and disinterested higher nature.

* See plate and note on p. 396 and 397.

28 September

*H*eavenly entities love harmony, and you can attract them with music, songs, and positive thoughts and feelings. Wherever they may be, luminous entities are drawn to the harmony and unity we create when we get together. They say to each other, 'How different these people are from other human beings who meet only to rage against their enemies, real or imaginary. Here are beings who have come together to create unity and harmony, to prepare the kingdom of God. Let us go to see them and help them.'

This state of harmony releases a fragrance that cannot be perceived by human beings, but which these luminous creatures delight in. And even the stars up in the heavens smile down on us and send us messages of love.

29 September

Imagine you want to go on a trip and you are hesitating between Nice and Moscow. Suppose you finally decide on Nice. From the moment your choice is made, your route is mapped out for you: the landscapes you will see, the stations you will pass through, the people you will meet – all these things are set. When you decide to travel to a certain destination, you must follow a pre-determined itinerary. It is not you who will create the roads you will travel over or the towns and villages you will pass through; their existence does not depend on you.

The only thing that depends on you is the choice of direction you wish to take. So, it is not we who create our destiny, whether good or bad; it already exists, and we simply travel towards it. But it is up to us to choose whether we want to go through quicksand, swamps, dangerous forests, or fertile plains and parks filled with flowers and birds. Every misfortune and every happiness already exist, and others have experienced them before us, they were created beforehand. It depends on us alone whether or not to visit them.

30 September

*T*he more firmly human beings are linked to the divine Source, the more they attract workers from heaven who come to help and support them. This is how people become strong, robust, radiant masters of themselves, and come to possess the powerful key of realization. Therefore, go in dread of doing anything that would repel these divine workers, for every mistake produces a nauseating stench that drives these invisible friends away.

When disciples place God above all else, when they pray and meditate so as to link themselves to Him, these heavenly workers let the waters of the river of life flow over them and illuminate them with their rays. If your soul were open to those beams of light, you would see before you a sublime world filled with beings of extraordinary splendour.

1 October

We have all been built in the same heavenly workshops, for the purpose of understanding and living the same divine realities.

In spite of this, human beings tend mostly to emphasize and cling to the differences and contradictions between them, and this leads to all kinds of misunderstandings and conflicts. Of course, they all agree that they have certain basic needs in common – to eat, drink, sleep, bring children into the world, and so on – but in every other area it is the Tower of Babel. Everybody says, 'To my mind it is like this … my opinion is this or that…' That is all very well, but they also need to consider the opinions of others. Each one is right from their own point of view, but the right of each makes for an overall state of conflict. 'Such is the way of the world,' they say. And the world goes from one conflict to the next because each individual wants their own 'right' to prevail.

2 October

Why are the trials that life sends to humans beneficial to some and harmful to others? Why do some people succumb or become malicious, while others, on the contrary, strengthen their willpower, their love and their light? In order to benefit from your trials it is not enough to be sturdy or strong-willed; thought and reason also have a part to play.

The first thing disciples must do when faced with a difficulty is to accept it and to tell themselves that, since they are children of God, they have within them the means to overcome it. Then they must look for these means, which are many and various. But the first thing to do is to accept the trial and not say, 'What? Something like this can't possibly be happening to me!' Well, you just have to accept that it is happening to you and try to draw from it the elements most useful for your evolution. This is why you should love your trials! But loving them does not mean that you should be so stupid as to go out and look for them. In any case, they will come your way without your looking for them. You must love them simply because that is the best way to get through them.

3 October

Do not think that you can enter the divine world if you do not work to bring yourself into harmony with it, for when you reach the border, you will be stopped by a customs officer who will ask you, 'What you have got in your suitcase, that is to say in your head? What awful thoughts are these? All I see is scheming, dishonesty and negative criticism. Now, show me what you've got in your heart. Oh dear, what is this selfishness and jealousy? And let's see your will. That is no better – what weakness and laziness! Well, know that you cannot come through like that.'

Indeed, just as there are countries that forbid the importation of certain products and objects, the kingdom of God is also a country in which weakness and destructive, negative thoughts and feelings are not accepted. Either you must get rid of them or you will be refused entry. Only those who fulfil the required conditions are allowed into the kingdom of God.

4 October

Whatever happens, always remember that God created humankind in his own image and that, however degraded or sunk in despair a person may be, it is impossible for them to be lost for good; they will always be held back on the edge of the precipice. It sometimes seems as though people are hurtling headlong toward oblivion, but in reality whatever they may do and however great the danger they may be in, they will always end up being saved. For the divine image is etched into the depths of their being and even when they seem to be lost beyond all hope, this image is like a powerful hand, holding them back and giving them the opportunity to turn back towards the light.

Remember this well: even if a person falls prey to forces that drag them to the abyss, nothing is ever irretrievably lost, because the Creator has fitted them with a type of safety lock, a spark that will testify to their divine filiation for all eternity.

5 October

*T*he cross represents the two principles, the masculine (the vertical line) and the feminine (the horizontal line) that come together to do their work in the universe. This work stems from a centre: the point of intersection of the two arms of the cross. This central point unites the forces; without it, they would be scattered over the disc formed by the cross as it starts to turn. For the cross spins, and as it spins, the arms trace the form of a circle. The cross in motion is a swastika. It can turn either to the left or to the right.

When the cross turns clockwise, it signifies the tightening of a screw to prevent the energies from manifesting themselves – they are held in and kept under control. This is the symbol of spirituality which restrains the forces of instinct. If the cross turns in the opposite direction, it means that the brakes are being released; the raw forces of instinct are let loose and the way is closed to the sublime powers of the spirit.

6 October

Suppose you have helped someone out, for example, you have given them money. Then, one day, you find that they did not deserve your help; so, you go and tell everyone what you did for them, and that they were not deserving of your kindness and so on. But why say all these things? If you go around complaining that you regret your kindness, you will simply destroy the good you have done. It had been recorded on high that you were due to be rewarded and now, by behaving as you have, you are erasing your good deed.

You must learn to turn a blind eye and forgive people for their failings. In this way you yourself will grow and anything you may have lost as a result of your kindness will later be given back to you a hundredfold. No matter what people do to you, never try to seek revenge; wait for heaven to pronounce itself in your favour, for sooner or later it inevitably will.

7 October

It takes three or four hours to completely digest a meal, but hunger is appeased much more quickly; within a quarter of an hour after a meal, you already feel restored and ready to go back to work. This shows that the most subtle part of our food is absorbed through the mouth while we chew. Only the coarser elements are assimilated by the stomach and intestines.

In the spiritual life, meditation is like the mastication of an idea. When you meditate or 'chew' on an idea for a long time, your superconsciousness receives a powerful flow of strength and energy that enables you to continue your work in the Lord's vineyard.

8 October

*J*esus said, *'Unless you become like children, you will never enter the kingdom of heaven.'* Do we really understand what it means to become like children, or why this is a condition for entering into the kingdom of God? Children are frail, vulnerable and trusting, and this arouses a protective instinct in adults. Jesus meant that we must be as children in relation to those who have surpassed us – the initiates and great masters – for they can take care of us, guide us, teach us and protect us.

It is a great mistake to think that because we are adults, we no longer need spiritual parents. This is precisely when the trouble really begins! The only way to enter the kingdom of God in joy, happiness and hope is to be as children in relation to those who are more advanced. Even if we are obliged to become adults here on earth, we must remain as children in relation to our divine parents.

9 October

We expect educated, cultured people to react in a measured, reasonable way in the face of difficulties, but more often than not, this is not the case. The slightest mishap throws them into pitiful states of anger or depression and they have no strength or willpower to rise above it.

All their education and learning is of no help to them. When will people understand that what matters is not to be a professor, an engineer or an economist, but to live? What good does it do them to flaunt the riches of others that they have gleaned from books? It is what they themselves have accomplished that they should display; and if they have nothing to show, they would do better to leave their book knowledge to one side and start doing what really matters: working to form their own character.

10 October

Situations cannot be resolved from below, by making decisions in the physical realm of matter; the impulse must come from above, from an exigency of the spirit. Those who do not know this law always try to intervene on the physical plane to change, move, demolish or rebuild things. But history shows that interventions of this nature are not lasting; after a while, a wave comes along and sweeps them all away.

Only that which is established on high, in the world of the spirit, is eternal; all the rest is ephemeral, transient. This means that when you want to bring about a lasting improvement in a given situation, you must rise to a great height and work in the world of the spirit. It is on that level that you must pray, formulate your requests and create images that will one day become concrete realities on the physical plane. If you are capable of setting in motion the luminous forces of the higher world, all obstacles will eventually be swept away and a new order of harmony and peace will reign on earth.

11 October

*M*any so-called spiritual people care only about their own interest, not what is in the interest of the universal collectivity! They have not yet understood that everything they do that is not in tune with the universal order, not only wreaks havoc, but it also backfires against them in the end.

It is not enough to do only what suits you, for you are not alone; there are other beings in the divine world who have something to say about what you do, and if you break the divine laws, you will be punished in one way or another. This is why it is important to devote a few minutes, several times a day, to attuning yourself with the luminous forces of the universe. It is not a waste of time, on the contrary, in doing so you will gain something very precious: you will be communicating with entities who come to help and support you.

12 October

*T*he human spirit is a child of God, an immortal, divine spark. It contains all God's powers, all his knowledge. Why then is the spirit so limited in its manifestations? Because of the physical body, which is still too crude, too grossly material. But this is no reason to despise or ill-treat the body, as Christians did for centuries. The body that God has given us is built with great wisdom and knowledge. It is the most perfect instrument we have, and if we learn to work with it every day and to refine and purify its matter, it will become capable of vibrating in harmony with the spirit.

Those who despise and neglect the body are as much in error as those who use it only to get as much sensual pleasure from it as possible. Only those who understand that the mission of the body is to manifest the hidden splendours of the spirit and to one day become living temples of the spirit are on the right path. How is it possible to imagine that the only function of this body given to us by God is to oppose the spirit, to extinguish the flame of the very spirit that makes us sons and daughters of God? What nonsense!

13 October

*I*magine you have before you two bottles of perfume. The two vessels are separate from each other but the fragrances they contain rise and mingle in the air. Human beings are like bottles of perfume: their bodies are separate, but by means of their thoughts, their soul and their spirit, they can meet with other human beings as well as with entities of the invisible world anywhere in the universe. By means of their quintessence, they touch and communicate with other spirits whose vibrations correspond to theirs.

And this is how we can touch and communicate with the Lord himself, for it is none other than a phenomenon of resonance. If you know this, it will help you to understand the reason for prayer, meditation, contemplation and identification. By striving to elevate yourself by means of your thoughts, you gradually manage to touch the universal soul and vibrate in unison with it. There is then a fusion between it and you: your weaknesses are driven out and the qualities of the universal soul enter into you so as to transform you.

14 October

The happiness most people seek is always associated with possessions: houses, money, honours, or perhaps a spouse and children. As long as they do not possess these things, they cannot be happy, and as their happiness depends on what they possess, the loss of those possessions is catastrophic. But if you come to understand what true happiness is, you will realize that it does not depend on an object, a possession or another human being; it is something that comes to you from above, and you are amazed to discover endlessly this marvellous inner state of consciousness... You are full of joy without knowing why you are happy. That is true happiness.

The day you manage to immerse yourself in the ocean of universal harmony, you will no longer need to look further for your happiness; you will be continually bathed in it. It is like breathing – breathing in and breathing out, breathing in and breathing out... Indeed, happiness is like the breath of the soul.

15 October

A valley symbolizes kindness, generosity, gentleness and fertility. It is in the valleys, not on the mountaintops, that we find trees, gardens, fruits, flowers, and towns inhabited by human beings. On high peaks, there are rocks, ice and barrenness.

Are you complaining that you are lonely? Well, go down into the valley where you will find abundance, where the rivers of love flow. The knowledge you have acquired on the peaks has to melt and form streams and rivers that will fertilize the valleys. Your intelligence must take you up to the mountaintops and your love must take you down into the valleys.

16 October

We can have doubts about many things but there is one law in which initiates never doubt: it is that we reap what we sow; and that if we do good, we will sooner or later harvest the fruits of our good deeds.

But we also need to know that the laws of the cosmos, unlike human beings, are not in a hurry; they march to a different beat. This is why the rewards often seem to be a little delayed, and the punishments too, for that matter! If you become impatient and angry because you feel that you have not received the reward you deserve, you will only complicate the situation. Why suffer and torment yourself? Sooner or later, these rewards are sure to come, so stop wasting your time waiting for them and you will feel much lighter and freer. Since you know that gifts are on the way to reward you, have faith. If you are bitter and incensed, it shows that you do not possess true knowledge.

17 October

When we see how different people are – how some are constantly driven to accomplish great things while others spend all their time on futile, petty trivialities – we are inclined to ask, 'Why is there such a difference? Where does it come from?' Well, it is simple: the former look upwards and compare themselves to all those who have surpassed them, and they take these people as models; whereas the latter are satisfied with points of comparison of such inferior quality that they find themselves to be quite good and they stop making progress.

In order to evolve, we need an example, a point of comparison, and that example must be the life and teaching of all the purest, wisest and noblest human beings.

18 October

*T*here are two sorts of knowledge. The first is the officially sanctioned knowledge that you receive in schools and universities, which provides you with the material things you need: a job, money, prestige and so on. However, this knowledge does not transform you, and you remain exactly the same with your anxieties and weaknesses. The second kind of knowledge, initiatic knowledge, may neither help you to find a position nor give you prestige, but it will transform you.

Of course, as human beings are mainly interested in material rewards, they seek the official kind of knowledge. Unfortunately this knowledge does not last. You cannot take book learning with you into the next world; it is yours for only this one incarnation. And what is one incarnation? A dream, a dream that lasts only a short while. But the initiatic knowledge that transforms us and teaches us the meaning of life is etched into our being for all eternity.

19 October

When everything is going well, people think only about their own affairs, their own interests and pleasures. It is when they are worried or unhappy that they suddenly think of God and wonder why He does not come and help them. They would like the Lord to realize there is a poor wretch here who is suffering, and come personally to console them and extricate them from this mess. As though the Lord had nothing better to do! Now I am not saying that God does not help us – He does – but we do not know how to receive his help.

Take the sun for example. The sun is very powerful – it makes the planets turn, it drives and vivifies them, and yet in spite of that tremendous power, if you do not draw back your curtains, it cannot enter your room. You leave your curtains closed and say, 'Come in, come in, dear sun!' And the sun replies, 'But I cannot.' Why not? 'You must open your curtains.' Yes, a mere curtain is enough to keep it out. If you understand this, you will draw back your curtains, the sun will enter and you will be flooded with light. The sun is a symbol of the Lord. Of course, the Lord is almighty, of course he holds the universe in his hand, but when it comes to opening a curtain he cannot do it; it is up to us to draw back our curtains so that he can come in and help us.

20 October

*H*uman beings have a tendency to seek only what gives them pleasure. But pleasure is not a reliable guide, and when we allow ourselves to indulge in it, the consequences are always unpleasant. While it is at first enjoyable to feast in a restaurant, when the time comes to pay the bill, it is not quite so pleasant. Why do people think that they can eat as much as they like without paying? Everything in life has to be paid for.

On the astral and mental planes as on the physical plane, there are markets, shops and displays of goods for you to choose from, but once you have served yourself you must pay. Faced with the thought of this payment, you should stop and ask yourself, 'Is it really worth it? Is not the price too high? After all, the pleasure is fleeting – there will soon be nothing left of it, and it will take me years to pay off my debts!'

21 October

*D*isciples seek fusion with the Deity through meditation and contemplation. The initiates of India have summed up this exercise in the formula, 'I am He', which is to say, God alone exists; I am only a reflection, a replica, a shadow; I exist only to the extent that I am able to become one with him.

In reality, we do not exist as creatures distinct from the Lord; we are part of him. This is why initiatic science teaches human beings the methods they must use to detach from their illusory images of themselves. When we say, 'I am He', we understand that we do not exist apart from God, so we strive to unite ourselves with him, draw close to him so that one day we shall truly be like him.

22 October

Life presents us with a series of problems to which we must find solutions. Those who, instead of making an honest attempt to solve their problems, try to sidestep them, soon find themselves faced with insuperable difficulties. Why? It is very simple. You have all been to school, have you not? And there, you studied grammar, mathematics and so on. For each subject you were given exercises to do. Take mathematics for example. Suppose that a student starts to skip the exercises of the first lesson; they will not have the elements they need to go on to the following lessons. What will happen to them? Their position will become more and more difficult and, at some point, they will no longer be able to manage. It is the same with the problems handed to us in life. Each correctly solved problem gives us the elements we need to tackle the next one under the best conditions because our efforts bear fruit: with each exercise, we become more perceptive, more patient and more resilient.

It is important to understand this very clearly; it is an illusion to think that you can behave like a truant pupil and skip the difficulties of life. The truth is that the problems you fail to solve will always be there, as roadblocks on your path, and you will soon find yourself faced with an insurmountable barrier.

23 October

*T*he science of the future will be the science of light and colours. For light – this seemingly weak and innocuous substance – is in fact the mightiest force in the universe. It is light that sets in motion the whole of creation.

Thanks to light, stones, plants, animals and human beings live, and worlds go round. This is expressed in the first words of St John's Gospel: *'In the beginning was the Word, and the Word was with God, and the Word was God. He was in the beginning with God. All things came into being through him, and without him not one thing came into being.'* Yes, the whole of creation stems from this primordial light: the Logos, the Word of God.

24 October

Thanks to the great truths and good influences they receive, and with the help of the angels, disciples of an initiatic school begin to remember the luminous world from which they have come and to which they must one day return. The greatest possible blessing for disciples is to remember...

They will also have to remember all the suffering they have endured as well as all the wrongs they have done and the debts they have incurred; for before they can free themselves from their karma, they will have to seek out those they wronged and make their peace with them and make amends for their wrongdoings. This is what awaits every disciple; this is what awaits each one of you. Sooner or later, you will be obliged to correct all the mistakes you have made and make reparation for all the harm you have done.

25 October

Life presents us with all kinds of temptations and if disciples have not learned to control themselves, they give in, and then of course they regret it because they sense that they have weakened and demeaned themselves. Most people consider it normal not only to be tempted but also to give in to temptation; they seem almost to think that this is why they came down to earth: to throw themselves headlong into whatever attracts them.

But disciples have a different point of view. They know that they have not been sent to earth to seek pleasure but to carry out a work on themselves. So, in order to avoid all kinds of disappointments, before rushing into some venture or other, they ask themselves, 'To do this or that will satisfy my desires to be sure, but what effect will my behaviour have on me and on those around me?' And they think it over. People who fail to ask themselves these questions are taken by surprise when unforeseen difficulties and problems arise. Well, they should not be surprised; they should have foreseen what would happen. It is always possible to predict the consequences of our actions.

26 October

Alchemists of old tried to find the philosophers' stone in order to turn base metals into gold. True, but an alchemist needs to be something more than a good chemist. A chemist needs to know only how to handle the right material elements to carry out a successful experiment, but alchemists must go much further than that – they will succeed only if they introduce spiritual elements into their work. Some alchemists who knew exactly the formula to use to produce the philosophers' stone and prepared all the necessary elements with the utmost care, still never achieved anything.

The process by which the philosophers' stone is made is more psychic and spiritual than physical, and those who wish to obtain it must study the virtues and achieve them within themselves. On this condition alone will matter obey them, and will they become true alchemists.

27 October

You will never really find happiness in love until you understand that love is not about the physical possession of another being.

True love can be found only in that subtle element that links you through the medium of another being with the whole universe, with the beauty of flowers, forests, springs, the sun and the constellations. Do not be in a hurry to close the physical gap that separates you from others, otherwise you will gradually lose this subtle world and will be left with only the prosaic material aspects.

28 October

*E*ach day you have the opportunity to attract spirits of light. Call them to you saying, 'Come, come my heavenly friends and dwell in me!' You can also add, 'Lord God, divine Mother, blessed Trinity, and all you angels and archangels, servants of God and servants of light, my whole being belongs to you; use me as you will for the glory of God and the establishment of his kingdom and his righteousness on earth.' To know how to pronounce these words is an act of true consecration.

If you do not learn to invite heavenly spirits to come to you, you need not be surprised if other kinds of spirits, which are far from heavenly, come and set up house within you. It is up to you to choose whom you want to 'inhabit' you. Angels will never come to you if you do not invite them but the devils have no such qualms; they will enter without waiting for an invitation!

29 October

*T*he mistake of many spiritual people is that they do not give their activity solid foundations. They venture in without preparation of any kind in the belief that they only need to ask and the invisible world will reveal itself to them; angels will be at their beck and call and all powers will be given to them. Unfortunately, this is not what happens.

A truly spiritual person spends twenty or thirty years preparing themselves, and then perhaps one day everything they have longed for will suddenly be theirs. In the spiritual realm, it is the preparation that takes time. But people never prepare themselves; they continue to allow their inner life to be cluttered up with every sort of futile concern. From time to time, of course, they supposedly meditate a little, and that is enough for them. Well it may be enough for them, but the truth is that it is not enough. There are some preliminary conditions to be met, and it is only once these conditions have been fulfilled that they will discover that spiritual work truly brings results.

30 October

*T*he image of a knight on horseback is full of meaning: the knight represents the spirit of man while the horse represents his physical body. Each one of us is then both horse and rider. And just as an equestrian must care for their horse, each of us must care for our bodies, keeping them healthy and making them work but without exhausting them. When something goes wrong, it takes a great deal of discernment to recognize whether the problem or weakness comes from your horse or from you, the rider. You are tired – is your fatigue physical or psychological? You feel hungry although you have just eaten and your physical body has had enough – who is hungry, you or your body? At another time, you have no appetite even though you have not eaten and your physical body must surely need food.

A contradictory situation like this can also arise with physical love: your body is surfeited and yet you still want more; or you have had enough but your body still clamours for more. Sometimes, despite using your spurs, your horse leads you down paths you do not want to venture. At other times, it is the horse that finds a way to save its master, having caught the scent of a danger the knight had not seen. This question opens up a vast field of reflection for you.

31 October

*B*ook knowledge is building material, a form of wealth – why should you not acquire it? It is the conclusions that you must be careful about. Indeed, you cannot trust the conclusions the scientists and philosophers have drawn from all the material they have at their disposal. When, after years of study and research, eminent thinkers and professors tell you that they have reached the conclusion that the universe is the work of randomness, that there is no order in the cosmos, that the soul and religion are inventions and should be rejected, that the earth is a battlefield where each individual must fight tooth and nail to avoid being devoured by their neighbour, and so on, listen to them out of curiosity if you want to, but do not let them influence you.

Besides, think of how many times the conclusions of scientists and philosophers have changed throughout the centuries. Why base your life on such shaky foundations? All knowledge must lead us to God, to an understanding of the meaning of life. If it cuts us off from God and from the meaning of life, it is better to leave it alone.

1 November

When the soul leaves the body during sleep, it is not idle; it travels, it contemplates immensity, it communes with celestial spirits and it strengthens its knowledge of love, wisdom and truth. When it returns to the body, it brings back the memory of all these riches, which it tries to imprint in the mind. Even if human beings are not immediately conscious of it, all these great truths leave an etheric imprint in them, that one day they will finally discover.

This is why it happens that certain sublime truths are suddenly communicated to you like a flash of light – you had undoubtedly already carried them in your subconscious for a long while. Until then, the time had not yet come for you to be aware of them, but suddenly there came that auspicious moment when your brain was in the right state of mind, and the truth burst forth. If you wish these experiences to happen more often, you must become much more disciplined in your life, for it is once human beings are in the habit of working to purify their physical body and make it sensitive that their soul can record the sublime truths more easily.

2 November

*J*esus said, *'Unless you die you shall not live'*. To die means to renounce your limited, human self in order to give way to the Lord, so that He may come and reign within you. You no longer cling to your own life; you wish to disappear, but on one condition – that it be the Lord who takes your place.

If you really insist, if you call to Him with the full strength of your love, He has to give in because you are using powers of the same nature as Him: the powers of love. He cannot say, 'Let's see, we have to think about this, and examine the way he lived in the past'. No, there is no longer any past; there is no longer anything; in the face of such a desire, everything else is erased. There is only your decision and the plea you have made today: to live the life of God.

3 November

Life is made up of exchanges between your inner and your outer worlds, but your inner world should always come first, for this is where you are continually immersed. You are not forever watching, listening, touching or tasting something outside yourself; but you are always with your inner self, your thoughts, your feelings and your conscious states.

As long as you give precedence to the outer world, you are heading for disappointment. Perhaps for a moment you might think you have a hold on something, but some time later you realize that there is nothing there, you have lost everything. Human beings are always looking for happiness, for a great romantic love, for fulfilment, but they must know that it is first within themselves, by organizing their inner world, that they will come to find them.

4 November

You are in the habit of eating while thinking of everything but food. This is why you cannot yet harness all the energies your food contains. You are distracted, your thoughts are scattered, you gulp your food automatically, and even though your organism feels sustained and invigorated, it has in fact only assimilated the crudest and most material elements.

You cannot imagine all the energies from which you could benefit if you only knew how to eat in silence, concentrating on your food in order to extract the etheric particles. From now on, try to think of nothing else while you are eating. At least for half an hour, leave everything aside and focus all your attention on your food, so as to extract the subtle energies that will help to fuel your spiritual life.

5 November

*M*ost human beings tend to work only for their own ends, but this solution is not ideal, for if misfortune falls on the collectivity it will fall on them too. As long as the whole collectivity does not live in peace and prosperity, the individuals within it are exposed to misery or misfortune. Whereas if the affairs of the collectivity prosper, all individuals benefit – even if adversity strikes one of them, all the others will come to help.

The foolishness of working only for oneself is very costly: suffering, wars and devastation. Unfortunately, since the time this has been going on, human beings still continue to work just for their own good, to the detriment of the collectivity. Everyone takes advantage, thinking that by looking after themselves, their future is secure. Well no! If misfortune befalls the collectivity, their happy little world crumbles around them, for they are part of this collectivity, and share in its vulnerability.

6 November

It is said in the sacred scriptures that God is 'faithful and true'. In other words that all your efforts to carry out His will, and to spread love and light amongst human beings are recorded, and one day you will be rewarded. When? This is the one thing which is hard to know, but you should not let it concern you. All you, yourself, have to do is work, and let heaven decide when, where, and how your efforts are to be rewarded. You must put everything in heaven's hands.

It is also written, *'Vengeance is mine says the Lord.'* This proves that neither do we have the right to avenge ourselves for injuries received. We must leave that to the Lord; He alone knows what punishment should be meted out to those who break the laws, and when and in what way you should be compensated.

7 November

So many people complain that they are starved of love! But why? They are surrounded by it. Love is spread throughout the universe, in the oceans, the rivers, the mountains, the rocks, the grass, the flowers, the trees, the earth, and especially in the sun. Love is a cosmic energy of untold abundance and diversity, and it is up to you to avail yourself of this abundance. Look at those plants which do not need to bury their roots deep into the soil to live, but instead draw water and sustenance from the atmosphere. Their organisms are different, better than the others.

Humans are not aware that they also possess spiritual centres which enable them to draw love from the atmosphere and from the sun. This is a pity as they do not develop these centres and so remain poor and unhappy. They must imitate the initiates who have worked to awaken their higher centres – the chakras – and who are able to draw on this energy that is spread everywhere in nature; they are happy, fulfilled, and live in plenitude.

8 November

God created the world by taking as its foundation the two principles, masculine and feminine. The law of construction always requires even numbers: 2, 4, 6 and so forth. That is why it takes at least two in order to work. Work is an association of at least two beings, two principles – each projects something of itself towards the other, and so there is a flow back and forth, a weaving between the two. The same thing happens within us too. We have a heart and a mind. The mind guides the heart, and the heart shares its impulses. This is how they build.

It is necessary for two to work together, but it is also difficult to do. This is why, in order to create good associations, we must be prudent and know how to keep certain distances. Do you think a bridge would be stable if its supporting pillars were too close together?

9 November

The only really effective method to be balanced and at peace is to enter into contact with the light. Of course, you will say you are not convinced because you have often tried it, without success, whereas with certain pills and potions the results are immediate. Well, you should know that your conclusions are mistaken.

You have not yet learned to work properly with light. You are content to spare it a thought from time to time, so of course this has no effect. Learn to vibrate in unison with it, to draw it in to you, to let it penetrate every cell in your body so as to make it ever more alive within you, and you will find that there is no power to equal that of light.

10 November

Many people wishing to embrace a spiritual life are confronted with the problem of meditation: they do not know how to concentrate. Why? Because they have never learned how to choose the subjects of their meditation, so they plunge into it blindly and without method. The first rule of course is to choose a subject of a spiritual nature, and the second is to find a subject that you like. It is your love of a subject that binds you to it. If you do not love it, you are like a stamp without glue – you will not stick to the object!

Beginners make the mistake of wanting to concentrate immediately on the most abstract philosophical and mystical subjects, such as truth, eternity, infinity, the Absolute, or the supreme Being. This is a mistake. Begin for example by focusing on a pure and beautiful image that you love, say of nature or of art. In this way your brain will gradually get used to concentrating and you will be able to meditate on more abstract subjects. In order to achieve results in the spiritual life, we must know how to harness the tremendous power of love.

11 November

You will never obtain great results in your spiritual life until you understand the magic secret of the law of affinity. Every emotion you experience is of a particular kind, and by virtue of the law of affinity, will awaken in space forces of the same nature that will make their way towards you. If your emotion is bad, you will attract negative forces; if it is good, you will draw blessings on yourself.

In this way, you can draw all that you desire from the great reservoirs of the universe, as long as you emanate and project thoughts and feelings akin to those you wish to attract. These thoughts and feelings determine the nature of the elements and forces that will be awakened far away, somewhere in space, and which sooner or later will make their way to you. The law of affinity is the greatest key, the greatest secret, the magic wand.

12 November

Make an effort always to see the good in others. Of course, you are going to say that if you cherish illusions about people, you are likely to be caught in a trap and pay dearly for it; the basis of human nature is bad, even religion says so, so why delude oneself?

Well, I would reply that your reasoning is incomplete and insufficient. You are dwelling on the evil in humans, and it is true that it exists. But we are all sons and daughters of God, we have a soul, a spirit, and though we do not see this divine spark at work very often, it is there, and if we give it favourable conditions there is always a chance it might manifest itself. In any case, it is certainly not by convincing ourselves that people are bad that we will bring out the divine side of their nature.

13 November

Who are the people all of humanity remembers with gratitude, those whom they praise the most? Those who have surpassed themselves, or those who have spent their lives in a selfish pursuit of enjoyment and pleasure? However much love and understanding we have for the human race, it cannot be denied that there exists a hierarchy among them, and that some have remained close to the level of animals, while others have reached great heights. These exceptional beings distinguished themselves from the others by the beauty and intelligence of their lives, and especially their service to others; they would not have been given this place of honour if they had done nothing good for the collectivity. Well, it is these magnificent beings, these benefactors of humanity, with their nobility, their integrity, and their disinterestedness, whom we must follow and take as our models!

When we study all these people who have won a place in history because of their genius, their high moral standing or their strength of character, we have to admit that there is a higher way of living, thinking and evolving, and another way, which makes humans revert to being animals.

14 November

The spiritual life is difficult, and can even be a risky adventure. Given the nature of the goal to be attained, it is impossible to reach it without effort, especially as the paths leading to it are not well travelled. These are untouched and steep paths, which skirt precipices, and where only a few initiates have walked. But the more difficult the task, the more glorious the success. Nature gives nothing if you do not make an effort.

Just look at competitive sports such as hurdling, skiing, or motor racing – are they easy? No, they are very dangerous. But if we accept these difficulties in sport, why should we not accept them in the spiritual life? In this, we want everything to be easy. But no, nature has placed obstacles on our path in order to see which of her children are able to embark on this enterprise and to triumph. Nature has strewn the path with difficulties. But with the splendour of victory before you, these difficulties should stimulate rather than discourage you.

15 November

For the majority of human beings, love is a feeling, a passion, a delirium, or a sickness – and an incurable sickness at that! No, true love is not like that at all. It is a state of consciousness attained by those who have walked the paths of self-perfection for a long time. It is the reward given to those who have understood that they will never be truly happy unless they draw nearer each day to the world of purity, harmony and light, which is the world of God himself.

And as God is the source of love, you receive the greatest gift of all: the feeling that you can expand your love to the whole world, to all creatures and all creation. You are able to stop focussing all your feelings or thoughts on one human being, in the hope that this person will satisfy all your needs, a hope that inevitably ends in suffering and disappointment. Each day, you draw closer to divine love, the only love that can fill your heart and soul.

16 November

*I*n order to maintain the balance of creation, the Creator has seen to it that each creature would have what it needs to survive. This is why, when humans fight and destroy each other, they are working against the Creator. Even if God created them different from each other, it was not so that they might use these differences as an excuse to fight. No one has the right to use God to justify their hatred for a particular race or people, or their wish to enslave certain social classes. All living beings come from God, and He suffers to see them tearing each other apart.

Humans have adopted a separatist philosophy in the name of interests which, they claim, are very lofty, but which are in fact prompted by their own egoism. Defence of these interests will eventually lead to humanity's downfall, for they go against the interests of the whole of creation. Yes, humanity's true interests are one and the same as those of the Deity. Only the merging of human interests with the interests of God will produce blessings for all.

17 November

Numbers are cosmic powers, active principles, which organize and control the equilibrium
of all that exists in the universe. This is why they
are situated very high in the hierarchy of spiritual
beings. It can be said that numbers are living
beings, albeit disembodied ones that belong to the
world of ideas. These intelligent entities, endowed
with the purest of virtues and intellectual powers,
work with God.

On the physical plane, numbers are symbolized by figures. Figures are the geometric
representations of these entities, of these forces
which make up the structure of the universe.
Our whole life, with our thoughts, feelings and
actions, is none other than a series of operations
involving the numbers 1 to 10.

18 November

*O*ften, when the disciples of a Master talk among themselves, they are astonished to find that their Master has not given the same advice to each of them. But we must understand that a Master's advice varies according to the person to whom it is given, and in relation to the period of their life.

For example, as long as you are not ill, a Master will tell you that to remain healthy it is enough to live a pure, intelligent and sensible life. But if you are ill, he will tell you to see a doctor, to take some medicine, or even to have surgery. When it is too late, these are the only means at your disposal. Similarly, to those who are not married he will say, 'Retain your freedom for as long as possible, and think carefully about what you are doing. Do not commit yourself too soon.' But if married men or women come to ask his advice he will say that in getting married, they have made a commitment, and must now assume responsibility for it to the very end. So a Master advises his disciples according to their mentalities, their needs, and their current situation.

19 November

*T*o have a good understanding of fire, we must also understand air, for air and fire complement each other. Air, with its coolness, has a regulating power over fire. We find the same phenomenon within ourselves. How? We are travellers, journeying through space; to fulfil our destiny we need both heat and cold. The heat is within us in that internal boiler, complete with fuel, which we carry with us to heat us from within, for it is very cold outside, and the way is long; we need to keep this inner fire burning. As for the cold, it comes from without; it is the air which regulates the temperature.

We could say that fire is love, and air is wisdom. Love is within us whereas wisdom is outside us, so that we may study it, contemplate it, and use it to regulate our inner fire.

20 November

When we sing in a choir, the high voices of the sisters and the deep voices of the brothers rise and fuse together over our heads, where they exchange extremely subtle elements. Your voice is imbued with your vitality, your perfume and your magnetism. Your voice is attached to you like a little kite on the end of a long string. Your voice leaves you and floats around above you, where it meets and blends with other voices before returning to you, amplified and enriched with all that it has received in this fusion.

So, when we sing, the masculine and feminine principles first do their work on high, and what they create then returns to us through our ears, and we all benefit from a chaste and divine exchange.

21 November

You feel justified in behaving according to your instinctive likes and dislikes. Well no, for in this way you are fuelling the conflicts around you, and wallowing on the lower levels of the astral plane. Do not believe, as so many do, that your feelings of affinity or antipathy stem from your intuition and clairvoyance about the people concerned.

No, these attractions or repulsions have a physical or biological origin, and are not at all spiritual. In the structure of their physical bodies or their faces, people have elements which are in affinity or in opposition to certain elements in your own biological make-up. This is why you feel attracted or repulsed by others. In fact, if you think about the question and take the trouble to examine it, you will probably find serious shortcomings in some of the people whom you find particularly endearing, and some very fine qualities and virtues in those for whom you feel a certain antipathy.

22 November

*E*ach day the Stock Exchange publishes the share index: some shares are up, others are down, those that are up today will be down tomorrow, and vice-versa. Share prices are a magnified image of what goes on in the world. At any given moment in history some shares are up while others are down. At certain periods, for example, the virtues of physical courage were extolled. The popular heros were those who fought fearlessly and with skill in tournaments, duels or wars. At other times, it was sanctity that was held in highest esteem. Much admired were those who were capable of giving up everything to devote themselves to God in silence and solitude, or to succour the poor, the sick and the persecuted.

Nowadays, it is the value of the intellect which is on the rise: the ability to reason and to acquire knowledge. But this will not last long – already another virtue is making an appearance: brotherhood. It is brotherhood which will encourage humans to act in a progressively more understanding and generous manner towards one another.

23 November

We often hear it said that thirteen is an unlucky number, and especially that there should never be thirteen people around a table. This is because the number thirteen does not like impurities, and fights against them. As it is a very active, dynamic number, it can harm those who do not possess the feminine qualities of goodness, love and gentleness with which to counterbalance its influence. You must be pure and full of love to feel at ease with the number thirteen.

On the physical plane, thirteen is linked to the cross ($1 + 3 = 4$), that is to say, to suffering and imprisonment. The cross is the cube unfolded in two-dimensional space, and the cube schematically represents restrictions, or prison. The number thirteen therefore, can bring 'bad luck' as we say. This bad luck is not due to the number thirteen, but to the way in which the individual is influenced by it. It depends on our physical and psychic make-up, on our elevation and our degree of evolution. Some fall ill, others start to reflect, and still others feel urged to act.

24 November

*M*atter must tend towards the spirit in order to become purer and subtler; and the spirit must tend towards matter in order to incarnate and manifest itself through it. In this way, the beloved crosses the divide that separates her from her loved one, who descends from celestial regions: they meet somewhere in space, and there they become one. When the spirit penetrates to the depths of a human being, it transforms the raw matter of the passions into beauty, purity, light, nobleness and love.

All of a disciple's work is summed up in this process: the descent of the spirit into matter. Whatever you do, whatever your pursuits, the books you read, your experiences in life, your exercises, they should all lead to what I summarize here for you in these words: the spiritualization of matter and the incarnation of the spirit.

25 November

When wicked, criminal people eat, how is it that this food which is divine, since it has been given by the Creator, does not make them better people? It is because they have transformed the food into their own nature. Whereas an initiate who eats the same food transforms it into light, love and goodness. It all depends therefore on the state of the person who is eating.

Wicked people are not improved by the food they eat – they even become more wicked. And those who are good become even better as they eat. It is a law: every creature assimilates their food into their own substance, and transforms it. This is why the initiates offer themselves in sacrifice to the Lord, so that they may be absorbed by Him. They know that as the Lord absorbs them, He will transform them and give them some particles of His light.

26 November

If I say that you should learn to walk with both legs, you will reply that you know that and have always done so. Well no, for I often see you hopping on one leg instead of walking. Sentimental people hop on the left leg – they never think too deeply – and the intellectuals hop on the right leg – their heart has dried up. You are all one-legged!

You think you know things, but you do not really know them since you have not put them into practice. All your life you remain poised on one foot, you even go out and about like that, hopping... But you should ask yourself, 'Why did nature teach us to walk by putting the left foot forward and then the right?' The answer is simple: it is because we must react alternately with our heart and our mind. We must learn how to alternate between the two principles, male and female, and recognize when we should switch polarity. Many difficulties and deceptions stem from not knowing how to walk on our two legs.

27 November

Having spent a certain amount of time immersed in a spiritual atmosphere, where they felt surrounded by light and warmth, disciples find themselves once again back in the ordinary world where they are obliged to mix with all types of people. After a while, they realize they no longer have the same faith, the same impetus. They feel themselves becoming heavy and dull again, and their ardour and love diminish. What has happened? Like a hot liquid that is then exposed to the cold, their temperature has changed.

This is a perfectly natural phenomenon. The teaching that disciples receive from a Master is like a liquid that is poured into a container. The contents are hotter than the surrounding air, and as they come into contact with this air they slowly loses calories and their temperature drops. But what is lost can be replaced. That is the purpose of meditation and prayer: to go to the Source in order to find the warm and luminous elements we have lost.

28 November

*I*t is said, *'This is eternal life that they may know You, the only true God...'* To know the Lord we must become one with Him. But fusion can take place only between objects or beings of the same essence. For example, take a small amount of mercury, and scatter it in droplets, then bring them close together again. Once again they unite to form a single drop. Now suppose that before gathering the droplets together again, you allow a little dust to fall on some of them: no matter what you do next, they will remain separate from the others.

Well, this is what happens when humans wish to unite with the Lord without having first purified themselves. As long as they remain impure, evil and dark, they cannot unite with the Creator who is all beauty, light and love. To rid themselves of the layers of impurity that are preventing this union, they must make certain sacrifices; they must learn to master themselves, to control themselves. Only on this condition can they begin to attune themselves with the divine vibrations and waves, and one day because of their pure life, they will even capture them.

29 November

Someone comes and complains to me, saying, 'I put the Teaching into practice; I am careful to follow your advice, and yet I still feel unbalanced, tense, verging on madness.' I reply to them, 'Well, to me, this is proof that you are mistaken in saying that you are carefully following the Teaching. You are probably giving free rein to something harmful within you, such as pride, your unbridled imagination or exaggeration in some form. Perhaps you are forcing things by wanting to see great spiritual results too quickly. None of this is consistent with the Teaching. So, do not blame the Teaching – it is you who are not going about it the right way.'

The Teaching is designed to help people find their equilibrium, to make them strong and happy, not to throw them off balance. If you are experiencing difficulties, you must look within you to see which laws you have transgressed. When the Teaching is properly understood and applied correctly, it can only harmonize your whole life.

30 November

*H*uman beings, like the universe itself, are governed by laws, and those who contravene these laws are crushed. Unfortunately, all over the world, we see only people who believe that with any thought whatsoever, any feeling or project, they will succeed. But no, they will come to a very bad end. You may say that it is not their fault; that nobody had taught them any better. Say, rather, that they never sought to be taught.

If we seek it sincerely, the light comes. If you seek an instructor, he will come. But most people are much more concerned with satisfying their whims and desires, and in seeking to do so, they come up against forces that break them. To date, no one has ever been able to oppose the powers of the universe or the waves and currents that flow through it. People say, 'I will defy all the laws. I will succeed, I will get what I want.' No, they will be crushed.

1 December

Collective does not mean fraternal, and a collectivity is not yet a brotherhood. A collectivity is a gathering of people who may have no bond between them. A village or a city is a collectivity, of course, but do all the people who live there know each other, do they love each other, do they work for one another? No, they are all separate, so this is not yet a brotherhood.

A brotherhood is a collectivity that has a broad, luminous consciousness, a collectivity whose members are united together and who work not only for one another but for the whole world. A true brotherhood is a universal brotherhood.

2 December

*S*ome people wonder why heaven does not decide to intervene and change the world. It could do so, of course, but without the consent and goodwill of human beings it would be of no use; they would not understand, nor would they appreciate this order established by heaven, and would soon destroy it.

Whereas if the desire for change comes from them, if they truly want to remedy the state of things because of what they have suffered and the lessons they have learned, the invisible world will set in motion other forces, other currents, other energies, and then true change will take place. But the impetus must come from human beings; they must decide together to work and ask the cosmic forces to intervene. If they do not insist, nothing will happen. The sublime Intelligences will never choose to get involved in the affairs of humans if the latter do not ask them to.

3 December

*M*ost people think that when they reach a certain age, their faculties will inevitably decline. Not only will they lose their teeth and hair along with the use of their legs, arms, eyes and ears, but they will also lose their memory and even their wits, and everybody believes this is normal. Well no, it is not normal. For the Initiates, in any event, old age is the best period of life, because years of searching and experience have not only brought them health, but also clarity, wisdom, peace and joy, and everyone comes to learn from them – even children are drawn to them and love them.

If the opposite opinion is prevalent in the world, it is because for most people, old age is indeed a very unhappy time as a result of the way they lived during their youth. If they spent their youth wasting their energies on foolishness and stupidities, what can they expect in old age?

4 December

*H*uman beings are what they are, and they cannot give what they do not possess. In order to give we must possess. This applies even more so in the field of art; in order to create we must carry within us the means to realize this creation, to express the splendour of the soul and the spirit. If we do not have anything within us, we will not create anything.

Some people present their so-called works of art, which are veritable monstrosities – one wonders where they found the idea. It is very simple: within themselves. We cannot produce anything divine if heaven does not dwell within us; and neither can we produce anything diabolical if we do not carry hell within us.

In order to give more than we are, we must come out of ourselves, rise, free ourselves and penetrate the higher realms to grasp a few particles of beauty or light that we will then give to others. This is the secret of divine art.

5 December

*T*he elements we absorb from food come from space, from the whole universe even. They come to us filled with cosmic life, and it is important for us to receive these elements with the awareness that they will form the substance of our physical and psychic bodies. We must therefore be extremely vigilant, for not only is this food imbued with universal life, it is also imbued with our words, feelings and thoughts. People who eat in anger while slandering or ranting about others do not realize that they are permeating the food with poisonous particles, and that in absorbing them, they are poisoning themselves.

In order to draw all the benefits from our food, we must work to introduce elements of light and eternity into it by means of thought.

6 December

A mother nourishes her child first with her blood, then with her milk. Symbolically blood, which is red, represents life, strength and activity; and milk, which is white, represents peace and purity; it is a principle of harmony that balances the instinctive tendencies represented by blood.

That is why children who are not fed with their own mother's milk lack something essential. Milk from other women or from animals does not contain the same elements for the child as its mother's milk. A mother who feeds her child with her own milk gives it the love and tenderness it so dearly needs for its development. That is why when she is angry or in a bad mood, she must not feed her child. She should wait until she calms down, because these negative states poison the milk, and the child then receives elements that can make it sick, both physically and psychologically. Mothers must be very vigilant and prepare themselves to always breastfeed the child in the best possible frame of mind.

7 December

When you have an important decision to make, you may sometimes be troubled because there are too many conflicting things churning inside of you – you feel pushed in one direction, then in another, then in a third and so on. In the midst of this confusion, you cannot see clearly, so it is not the time to make a decision, as the conditions are ripe for you to make mistakes.

It would be better to take your time so as to calm yourself and let things quieten down, for it is only in the silence of thoughts and feelings that you will receive the answer from your higher Self, your spirit. This silence is the source of clarity, transparency and certainty, and you need this silence to make the right decisions.

8 December

*H*ow many of you are in the habit of taking note of the truths that could help you? You read books, you listen to lectures but instead of meditating on the solutions that you have been given, you let everything fade away. That is why when the moment comes to face difficulties and trials, you do not recall that you have received the means to overcome them.

Yes, some people will hear or read about the truths that can save them four or five times, but they do not make a note of them, they forget everything. It is as if they had never read or heard a thing – they are always struggling with the same problems. Those who do not have a work method are really to be pitied for they will never get anywhere in life.

9 December

From the moment you enter into a state of harmony, a whole series of chemical reactions is activated in your body, and your physiological processes start to run more smoothly. You must try to experience the power of the spirit, the power of the soul, of thought and feeling on your body.

So many people become unhinged because they endlessly harbour chaotic feelings! They have not understood that these feelings are a formidable force that is destroying them, and they continue to seek the cause of their illnesses elsewhere. They must finally understand that their feelings are making them sick and that they must stop fuelling them. They should at least embrace the idea of having positive feelings in order to get well!

10 December

You are holding a photograph of the man or woman you love – why must you sully and limit this being by projecting sensual desires onto them, by thinking about how to enslave them, to make them yours? On the contrary, you must entrust them to the Lord, to the divine Mother, saying, 'Here is your daughter, your son, bless this person and inspire in me the best thoughts so that I may help them in their evolution.'

And if you should happen to stroke their head, their hair, rather than seeking only pleasure, think of doing something for their good and say, 'May God bless you, may light reign in this head, and may all the angels come to dwell in it.' In this way, you transform your love: it will no longer be strictly sensual but will become an extraordinary feeling the like of which you have never known before.

11 December

You do not yet know the true beauty of a human being because you look no further than the form. If this form is harmonious and attractive, you exclaim, 'How beautiful!' But beneath this form there is still more to see: the expression, the emanations that come from within this being, the life that flows. And if you were able to go even further and see the spirit of this being, which lives in heaven, you would discover even greater beauty. But actually, the splendour of the spirit is far too subtle to find physical expression.

True beauty cannot be described; it is life, a life that springs forth, that emanates... You have, for example, a diamond struck by a ray of sunlight – you are dazzled by the burst of colour that you see appear. This is true beauty. And the more a person manages to emanate such beauty, the closer they draw to true beauty.

12 December

What happens when a speaker takes the stand at a conference? All eyes are upon them, everyone's thoughts are focussed on them, and a link is established with the audience. Of course, if the speaker puts forth anarchic ideas, if they incite their listeners to anger and hatred, this link is not really advisable.

But let us suppose this lecturer is an Initiate who speaks to you of magnificent things: in his perpetual desire to link you to another centre above him, the unity that you form as you look at him, uniting with his thinking and becoming one with him thus takes on a deeper meaning, it becomes truly creative. All speakers should be aware of this fact so as to understand what miracles they can perform through the power of speech.

13 December

*T*he Caduceus of Hermes summarizes the human being. The staff represents the spinal column, and the two entwined snakes represent the two currents that descend from the brain's right and left hemispheres. In fact, these are not two snakes wound around the magic wand, but a single one that is polarized. The staff always represents the masculine principle, and the snake or the spiral, the feminine principle that curls around the masculine principle in order to exalt the powers contained within it. The staff is an expression of the mental plane, whereas the snake – polarized into positive and negative – is an expression of the astral plane, through which flow the two currents: one ascending, the other descending.

The Caduceus of Hermes therefore symbolizes both the masculine principle (the wand) and the feminine principle (the snake polarized into positive and negative because the feminine principle is always expressed by the number two). It represents a human being with all the faculties they must develop in order to manifest divine power.

14 December

Only those who love each other truly know what silence is. The strength of their feelings brings them a fullness that no words can express; this is why they live a life of the greatest intensity without there being any need to speak. However, more often than not, this love does not last. People do not know how to make it last; one day, the silence that sets in between them is one of indifference, resentment, and even hatred. Why? Because their love for each other was selfish and limited – they focussed solely on each other, they immediately gave each other the best they had.

If you wish your love to be enduring, you must see to it that you renew yourself by seeking to acquire new riches, new beauty and new light every day.

15 December

Make all your activities converge towards a single goal: to reach perfection, and then you will activate powers within you that will transform you to the depths of your being.

The professional activities of human beings generally affect them only superficially. All the powers bestowed upon them by the Creator cannot be awakened by going to the factory or the office, working in a laboratory, practising politics or teaching children, unless they also work with their thoughts, feelings and willpower to give these activities deeper meaning, touching the roots of their being. So, from now on, make up your mind to begin this work – the one and only work. Try to develop a taste for it, never letting a day go by without setting in motion beneficial forces in and around you, and you will see the results!

16 December

*T*he past is inscribed on our hands, and this is what chiromancy studies; the present is inscribed on our face, which is what physiognomy studies; and the future is inscribed on our skull, which is what phrenology studies. However, this does not mean that each of these sciences does not contain certain elements of the other two.

Our face reveals the present, who we are now. Our hands reveal our past. As for our skull, it reveals our future, because everything is contained in our head as potential waiting to be worked on, developed and organized. So, to find out where you stand right now, look at your face. To know your past, look at your hands. Finally, to find out what you have yet to express in the future, study your skull.

17 December

*T*he majority of spiritual people believe that having chosen the most sublime ideal, they will be able to achieve it without encountering any obstacles. No, that is impossible. In order to reach the goal, we must always travel paths strewn with pitfalls. Even Jesus, after his death, passed through hell before returning to his Father. And on the Sephirotic Tree,* to go from *Malkuth* (the earth) to *Tiphareth* (the sun) you must pass through *Yesod* (the moon), in whose lower region lies every danger.

When you want to go towards heaven, you are first assailed by hell, for you cannot realize a luminous, divine idea without meeting with opposition, struggle and suffering. If someone succeeds in a great, divine endeavour at once, it is because they have already suffered a great deal in previous incarnations and now have the qualities to succeed immediately in this incarnation.

* See the note and figure on pp. 398-401

18 December

*Y*oung people need activity, they want to do something, but to begin with, they do not really know what. And later on, when they have a better idea of what they want, they have no clear notion of what adventures their desires will lead them on.

So they need a light to show them where to go; then whatever they undertake will prove beneficial. But this light can be found only in an initiatic school where they will be taught truths that are not taught elsewhere, certainly not in universities. Without this initiatic science, human beings are condemned to make one great discovery when they leave the earth, indeed, one dazzling discovery, which is that they have understood nothing about life. This is quite a discovery, but it is of little use to them at that moment, and they take it with them to the other side. So, I would say to young people, 'Ask for just one thing in life: that Providence places you before the truths of initiatic science so that you may be saved.'

19 December

*T*rue adepts of initiatic science do not rely on anything external; they know that God has deposited within them every possibility, every form of wealth, and every substance from every laboratory. And that is where they must look for them. Of course, this is a long-term undertaking that requires daily effort, but it is worth it.

The nourishment you obtain from the sublime realms of the soul and the spirit satisfies you for days and days because on the divine plane, there are elements of such richness that if you manage to taste them but once, the feeling of fullness they bestow upon you never leaves you. Nothing can take this sensation of immensity and eternity away from you.

20 December

Whenever someone gives in to a base desire, they shackle themselves and become a slave; this is why we find so many slaves on earth. Even if human beings appear to be free, the truth is that inwardly, they faithfully obey a master: their lower nature, which exploits them mercilessly. In order to justify themselves they say, 'I couldn't help myself', without thinking that from the moment they utter this phrase, it is precisely because they are already enslaved, there is someone else inside who has taken control and who is holding tightly to the reins.

Someone who is free never says, 'I couldn't help myself', because these are words of capitulation, a calling card on which is written, 'I am weak, I am nothing.' 'How can that be? On my card it says that I am the president of this, the director of that, inspector of such and such' Ah? Perhaps, but an Initiate reads something completely different.

21 December

*S*agittarius symbolizes someone in whom reason has triumphed over the dark instinctive forces. This idea is also expressed by the mythological figure of the Centaur, which has the upper body of a man mounted on the lower body of a horse.

Human beings are made up of two natures: lower and higher. They cannot rid themselves of their lower nature, but must learn to control it so as to put it to work. What is more, illustrations of the Centaur or Sagittarius show the horse's body in motion, galloping. But this motion is not without purpose or direction, it serves a well-considered action, expressed by the bow held by the Centaur who is ready to shoot an arrow. You know what mastery it takes to draw a bow and aim true. So Sagittarius represents someone who places the movements of their lower nature – represented by the galloping horse – at the service of an ideal, symbolized by the arrow that flies precisely to its mark.

22 December

Wherever you go, whether to the mountains, the forests, the lakes or the seaside, if you wish to demonstrate that you are children of God who aspire to a more subtle and luminous life, you must show that you are conscious of the presence of the etheric creatures who live there.

Approach them with respect and reverence; begin by greeting them, then tell them of your friendship and love, and ask for their blessings. Enchanted by your attitude, these creatures, who perceive you from afar, prepare to shower their gifts upon you in the form of peace, light and pure energy. You will feel bathed and enveloped in the love and wonderment of these spiritual beings; when you return to the valleys and towns, you will bring all these riches back with you, as well as revelations and ideas that are broader and more profound.

23 December

The kingdom of God cannot be realized on the physical plane before being realized in the intellect, in our thoughts. Once realized in our thoughts, it will descend into the heart, into our feelings, at which point it can finally be expressed by deeds. For such is the obligatory process of realization in matter: thought – feeling – action.

One day, the kingdom of God will be realized tangibly in matter. But first, it must enter our thoughts as an idea. And we can see that the process has already begun. Thousands of people in the world – actually many more than you think – nourish within themselves the ideal and love of the kingdom of God. And in some of them, the kingdom of God is already making inroads into their thoughts and desires. In their conduct and way of life, the kingdom of God has in fact already been achieved. The kingdom of God is first and foremost a state of consciousness, a way of living and working, and once this state of consciousness has become generalized, the kingdom of God and His justice will truly come down to earth.

24 December

Silence is the highest region of our soul, and the moment we reach this region, we enter into cosmic light.

Light is the quintessence of the universe. It passes through and permeates everything we see around us, and even that which we do not see. And the goal of the silence we strive to instil within us during our meditations is fusion with this light which is vibrant and powerful and which penetrates all creation.

25 December

*T*he birth of the divine Principle within you is an inner event about which there can be no mistake. As if heaven were there, open before you, you feel the presence of another being who supports, enlightens and protects you, and brings you great joy. Even in the direst of circumstances, when you are at your lowest point, you feel that it is there and that you are helped.

Yes, it is the feeling of a presence, a connection that is never severed. It is as if you had with you the flame of a lamp that never goes out. When you have need of it, it can provide you with all the light and warmth you desire, but in the meantime, even if you do not use it, it is always there at your disposal.

26 December

*T*he marriage of spirit and matter, of heaven and earth, is celebrated each and every day. So, be sure you are invited to take part in the festivities given by the Lord, the divine Mother and all the angelic hierarchies.

Do you imagine that your wish to participate in these festivities is enough to gain admission? Well, no, because in order to be admitted, you must fulfil certain conditions. And if you simply show up without being prepared, you will suffer exactly the same fate as the man mentioned in one of Jesus' parables – he had presented himself at the feast without having clothed himself in ceremonial dress and he was not received. This dress symbolizes the qualities that must be developed for admission to the table of the feast. Perhaps you will not be invited to sit at the right-hand of the master of the house, but this does not matter. Even if you are at the other end of the table, it is worth having a small place so that you can attend the feast.

27 December

Without them knowing it, human beings are repositories of all the knowledge in the universe. This knowledge, which is deposited very deep inside them, lies there without moving, without vibrating, because it has not been given the conditions to do so; it therefore remains inaccessible to them for a very long time.

You may say, 'But how can that be?' Oh, it is a very long story. Since leaving the womb of the Eternal and descending into matter, human beings have travelled a long way through time and space. This has often amounted only to some adventures and dramatic episodes, over the course of which they experimented and gained new knowledge, but they also lost a great deal of the light and knowledge they originally possessed. Or, to be more precise, this knowledge was gradually covered by an accumulation of opaque layers. In order to regain possession of this knowledge, they require certain conditions that they can find only in an initiatic school.

28 December

When we lack inspiration, we are like a tree in winter, but we should know that inspiration comes periodically just like the flowering of a tree – when the conditions are right, in the spring. It is therefore up to us to create the conditions of spring in our soul. How? By means of love.

It is love that creates spring within us, but not just any kind of love, spiritual love. The spirit is not willing to be directed, it blows where it will, as it is said in the Gospels, *'The wind blows where it chooses, and you hear the sound of it, but you do not know where it comes from or where it goes.'* But by means of love, we create the conditions for its coming.

29 December

In so far as a person takes part in divine life through their higher Self, they also participate in the work of God. At the moment, they cannot yet realize what is happening in the higher spheres of their being, because they do not have a conscious link with these spheres, and so this is precisely what they must work on.

The divine Spirit dwells within us and if we must place ourselves in its service, it is not to strengthen it, for the Spirit is already powerful; it is not to instruct it as it is omniscient; nor is it to purify it as it is a spark. Our only preoccupation must be to clear the way for it, and then the divine Spirit will gives us its light, its peace and its love.

30 December

Royalty is tied to the notion of self-mastery. A king who governs others but has not learned to govern himself is not really a king, but a slave. The true king is someone who knows how to master himself.

When a disciple is committed to the ideal of escaping the domination of their selfish tendencies, and controlling and directing their thoughts and feelings, they are on the path to royalty. Then, the spirits of nature bow at their passing, whispering among themselves, 'Look, a king is drawing near', and they celebrate them, they joyously crowd around them. For a fluid of great purity emanates from their royal blood, imbued with curative, soothing influences like a divine source that flows and brings life to all the beings nearby.

31 December

*O*nce you have entered an initiatic school, know that you have a duty to fulfil, the duty to transform yourself so that all those you meet will marvel and decide to follow your example.

How can people fail to see the beauty of this endeavour? Finally make up your mind to begin work on yourself of which you will one day be proud. Pride, in fact, is one of the least prevalent sentiments among human beings. When you meet people, what strikes you is that they are not proud; deep down inside they feel that what they have done is not great. Outwardly, they pretend to be something, but inwardly you sense that they are not as happy and sure of themselves as they would like to appear. To be proud of yourself because you feel that you have accomplished your task, that you have done all that you could do, is an extraordinary state of consciousness.

There is no greater happiness than to be able to leave the earth with this feeling of pride – the pride of a job well done.

The Night of Wesak

*E*ach year, in the Himalayas, during the night of the full moon in May, the ceremony of Wesak takes place.*

The full moon in May is doubly under the influence of Taurus: the sun has been in this sign since 21 April, and the moon is also exalted in this sign.** Taurus represents prolific nature, fertility and abundance, emphasized further by the fact that it is the home of Venus, the planet of creation. So the full moon in May offers the best conditions for working with the forces of nature to attract heaven's blessings for the harvest and livestock, but also for human beings. For, if humans know how to attract the beneficial effects circulating through the cosmos at this time, they too can benefit from them, not only on the physical plane but also on the spiritual plane. This is why, by means of meditations, prayers, chants and magical invocations, initiates seek to create lines of force in space that will attract energies, which they send to all beings who are vigilant, awakened and capable of participating at this event.

---

* Wesak is the festival of the Buddha. In Tibet, it is celebrated in the valley of Wesak.

** Some years, when the sun is in Taurus, the full moon takes place in April.

There are places on earth that are more favourable than others for this cosmic work. The site where the ceremony of Wesak takes place is the most powerful of all. Some initiates go there physically, others by astral projection. But it is possible for everyone, including you, to take part in thought. During this night, you must not keep any metal object on you, since metal is not a good conductor of the waves of energy that come down from spiritual regions. But the only truly essential condition for being admitted to this festival is harmony. So be careful not to hold onto any negative thought or feeling towards others, and find the right inner attitude that will allow you to receive the blessings that the initiates send to the children of God on this night.

INDEX

B

Beauty
- tears of wonder are infused with divine power, 7 Mar.
- an Initiate looks at your soul, 5 Apr.

True **Beauty** is a life that springs forth, that emanates, 11 Dec.

Blessing, the greatest – remembering the luminous world from which we descended, 24 Oct.

Blessings
- open yourself up to heaven in order to receive them, 9 Apr.
- produced when the interests of humans and God merge, 16 Nov.

Body
- stop identifying with the physical body, 12 Feb.
- the physical body changes under the impulse of a feeling, 10 Apr.
- the physical body's mission is to manifest the splendours of the spirit, 12 Oct.
- caring for our physical body the way a rider cares for its horse, 30 Oct.
- purifying our physical body so that the soul may record the sublime truths, 1 Nov.

Breastfeeding – mothers must do so in the best possible frame of mind, 6 Dec.

Brotherhood – a community that possesses a luminous consciousness, 1 Dec.

C

Caduceus of Hermes, the – it symbolizes the two principles, 13 Dec.

Care and wisdom solve many problems, 28 May

A living **Cell** contains infinite possibilities for the future, 25 Jan.

Centre, the – the closer we get to it, to the spiritual sun, the more we feel its light, 14 Jan.

Centre or the summit, the – reach it in order to obtain every possibility, 28 Jan.

Chakras – the means by which the initiates draw on the love found throughout nature, 7 Nov.

Change – enjoy outer variety without changing direction, 12 May

Changes in the world must come from human beings' desire for them, 2 Dec.

Character – what really matters is working to form our character, 9 Oct.

Children
- do not spare them every difficulty, 4 Feb.
- we must remain as children in relation to our divine parents, 8 Oct.

Choir, the – a fusion of the voices of the masculine and feminine principles, 20 Nov.

Circle with a point, the – a structure that exists everywhere, 27 Feb.

True **Clairvoyance** is found in our heart, 23 Feb.

Collective life – it has only solved material problems, 14 Feb.

Collectivity, the – everyone benefits if they work for the good of the collectivity, 5 Nov.

Communion – a fundamental act of life through the food we eat, 31 Mar.

Concentration – a method to learn how to meditate, 10 Nov.

Consciousness
- expanding it by entering the immense community of beings, 1 June
- a screen that reflects both the higher and lower nature, 27 Sept.

Consecration – learn to invite the heavenly spirits, 28 Oct.

Contemplation – opening yourself up to come into contact with living nature, 17 June

Cosmic Law – we reap what we sow, 16 Oct.

Criteria to recognize whether it is really the Master who speaks to you inwardly, 27 June

Cross, the – it can turn to the right or to the left, 5 Oct.

D

Decisions – making them in calm and silence, 7 Dec.

A **Decree** – devoting one's life to something useful, 10 Sept.

Demands – the whole body makes demands, but there must be a head in charge, 7 May

Demeaning tastes – instead of struggling directly against them, kindle a love of light, 26 Mar.

Baser **Desires** – sacrificing them to feed our inner fire, 24 Apr.

Destiny
- a person's destiny is determined by their attitude towards heaven, 26 Jan.
- human beings are predestined to return to the bosom of the Eternal, 7 Feb.
- it can be changed by the idea of universal brotherhood, 6 Sept.
- we travel towards it, 29 Sept.

Diamond – the image of an Initiate who has become a pure, sparkling light thanks to his trials and love, 25 Apr.

Difficulties
- they can only be resolved with faith, 3 May
- they give us the means to strengthen ourselves, 19 July
- remember the solutions that have been given to us, 8 Dec.

Disappointments – keep your faith, hope and love, 2 Sept.

A true **Disciple** has learned to ascend and descend, 3 Sept.

Disciples – thanks to their Master, they are in contact with a higher principle, 20 Mar.

A **Drop of water** – each human being can be compared to one, and must sacrifice them self, 22 Jan.

Drugs – the cry from a soul starved for infinity, 25 June

Dying – renouncing our human self in order to give way to the Lord, 2 Nov.

E

Earth, the – cultivate it according to initiatic rules, 14 June

Ecstasy – when the soul melds with the Cosmic Spirit, 10 Aug.

Educating – a mother must first establish contact with heavenly life, 17 Mar.

Education – letting go of ideas that are harmful to society, 9 Aug.

Efforts – working on our inner matter gives life another flavour, 10 May

Enemies – paralyzing them with a single gesture, glance or word, 29 Mar.

Entities
- our thoughts and feelings attract spirits of darkness or spirits of light, 26 Aug.
- heavenly entities are drawn by harmony, 28 Sept.

Equilibrium – uniting your divine ideal with earthly reality, 6 Mar.

Etheric Creatures – show them that you are aware of their presence in nature, 22 Dec.

Evil
- the Initiates' stepping stone to great heights, 2 Mar.
- only God can make good take the place of evil, 4 Mar.
- project light to drive out evil, 11 Mar.

Evolution
- achieving the synthesis of form and spiritual forces, 22 Feb.
- the Initiates' stepping stone to great heights, 2 Mar.
- a person's evolution can be determined by the intensity of the light emanating from them, 8 May

Evolution is measured by the intensity of a person's life, 25 Mar.

To **Evolve** we must compare ourselves to the wisest beings, 17 Oct.

Exchanges – knowing how to make them so as to experience a subtle and poetic life, 12 July

F

Failures – accepting that we have much to learn, 19 Aug.

Family is determined according to your merits, 29 June

Family is not an end but a point of departure, 26 June

Feelings more than thoughts drive people to act, 5 Feb.

Feelings – they have the power to destroy us or to heal us, 9 Dec.

Fire is the food of the Initiates: Ahura-Mazda, 16 Feb.

Five senses – the five senses are also useful in our dealings with others, 6 Feb.

Food
- drawing energy from it by the way in which you eat, 12 Apr.
- extracting subtle energies from it in order to fuel our spiritual life, 4 Nov.
- introduce elements of light into it by means of thought, 5 Dec.

Formulas – said aloud three times to reach the three worlds, 21 May

The **Freedom** of God infuses those who want to serve Him, 5 July

Fruits – correspondences with the three fundamental virtues, 30 July

Fulfilment – very few things are truly necessary to find it, 25 Feb.

Fusion with the Lord – we must first purify ourselves, 28 Nov.

Future – preparing for the future by taking care to do everything properly today, 28 Feb.

Our **Future** depends on the regions towards which we are heading, 8 June

G

Gifts
- entities that dwell within a being and manifest themselves through them, 30 June
- they must be used to enlighten other beings, 21 Aug.

By **Giving**, we become richer, 11 Jan.

God
- our point of departure and our destination, 13 Apr.
- to draw closer to the spiritual sun, read the book of nature, 20 Sept.

Good deeds – never regret having done them, 6 Oct.

Good and evil are harnessed together to keep the wheel of life turning, 26 Feb.

H

Happiness concerns the whole of our being, 7 Sept.

Happiness
- we will find it by developing brotherly relations, 11 Apr.
- the selfish pursuit of happiness will get you nowhere, 18 June
- do not asked to be loved, just continue loving, 6 July
- love without waiting to be loved in return, 24 Sept.
- a state of consciousness that does not depend on any object, 14 Oct.

Heart and mind – learning to alternate between the two principles, 26 Nov.

Heaven and earth – meeting certain conditions to be admitted to their wedding, 26 Dec.

High Ideal, the – impossible to achieve without encountering obstacles, 17 Dec.

Higher Self – a sublime being who wants to know itself through matter, 5 June

Higher senses, the – hearing and sight leave human beings free, 27 May

Holidays – the best form of rest is spiritual work, 28 July

Hope – wisdom that knows how to use the past and the present to shape the future, 29 May

Hope, faith, love correspond to form, content and meaning, 11 May

Horoscope – thought is dynamic when Mars and Mercury are well aspected, 4 Aug.

Human beings
- all the sciences reside within them, 17 Feb.
- the four categories of knowledge, 20 Feb.

Human beings are placed between matter and the spirit, 16 May

Human beings are destined to return to their heavenly Father after many incarnations, 10 June

I

'I am He' – a method for detaching from illusory images of ourselves, 21 Oct.

Idea – a sublime idea leaves the door wide open to all the spirits of light, 9 Jan.

Ideal
- by always adhering to a high ideal, you become a source of help to others, 30 Mar.
- the highest ideal is to model oneself on the sun, 1 May

Identify with light and love so as not to lose them, 12 Mar.

The **Image of God** in man prevents people from losing themselves, 4 Oct.

Imagination – purifying one's mental body so as to begin to see the invisible world, 24 Jan.

Improve yourself in order to improve the quality of your seeds – your thoughts and feelings, 8 Jan.

Improving a situation by rising up to the world of the spirit, 10 Oct.

Improving oneself – rising up to contemplate a reality that surpasses us, 19 Apr.

Improving your future by preparing to become the master of your destiny, 25 May

Incarnations – even the greatest beings must work to regain their knowledge, 15 Feb.

Initiates
- true children of God who never leave His side, 8 Apr.
- a true mirror by which to know oneself, 8 Aug.
- the first to be in unison with light, 12 Aug.

Initiates wish to be absorbed and transformed by the Lord, 25 Nov.

Initiatic knowledge is etched into us for all eternity, 18 Oct.

Initiatic school allows us to rediscover universal knowledge, 27 Dec.

Initiatic school – the symbolic return to a divine order, 6 Jan.

Initiatic teaching gives us the means to improve our future incarnations, 24 Feb.

Inner discomfort
- find the cause of it and dispel it with light, 1 July
- caused by chaotic thoughts and feelings, 2 July

Inner world – organizing our inner world so as to find fulfilment, 3 Nov.

Intelligence – improving it by improving one's way of life, 14 Sept.

Intuition – true intelligence, 16 Sept.

J

Joys – find the best, noblest and most beneficial ones, 18 Aug.

Justice – human justice or divine justice, 5 Sept.

Divine **Justice** does not manifest itself immediately, 18 Sept.

K

The **Kingdom of God**
- for it to come, a huge crowd must ask for it, 2 May
- we have nothing to lose by working towards its realization, 11 Aug.

The **Kingdom of God** must first manifest itself in our thoughts and ideas, 23 Dec.

Knowing a being by their subtle emanations, 11 Sept.

Knowing oneself – freeing oneself from one's denser bodies in order to live solely in one's divine bodies, 26 July

Knowledge – manifesting it through one's behaviour, 24 July

Knowledge must be enlivened by love and light, 15 July

Knowledge must lead us to an understanding of the meaning of life, 31 Oct.

L

Land of the living, the – people who manage to purify themselves can inhabit it, 8 July

Law of affinity, the – each thought and feeling will awaken forces of the same nature in space, 11 Nov.

Laws of nature, the – if we transgress them, nature strikes back, 23 Apr.

Laws of the universe
- to understand them, observe them over a long period of time, 14 Mar.
- those who go against them are crushed, 30 Nov.

Liberation – the soul needs the help of fire to free itself, 25 Sept.

Life
- it is by means of the spirit that life will be truly transformed, 27 Apr.
- always presents us with different problems to solve, 23 May
- dying to the lower life in order to live the higher life, 23 June

Life and death – life in one region is death in another, 14 May

Life of the soul and the spirit that we must rediscover, the, 11 Feb.

Light is the mightiest force in the universe, 23 Oct.

Light
- we can amplify it by taking part in its work, 15 Jan.
- seek it out before throwing yourself into endeavours, 30 Apr.
- those who work for the light awaken the forces of darkness, 3 Aug.
- there is no power equal to it, 9 Nov.

Likes and dislikes have a physical origin and are not at all spiritual, 21 Nov.

Link with God, the – never stop drawing from the Source, 11 July

Linking ourselves to divine source to attract workers from heaven, 30 Sept.

Living – the higher way or the animal way, 13 Nov.

Love
- do not cut it off from universal life, 18 Mar.
- energy that comes from on high and which must return there, 21 Mar.
- devote it to heaven, otherwise hell will come, 21 July

Love is a force that acts on you and gives you immense possibilities, 19 June

Love is symbolized by the fertile valleys, and intelligence, by the peaks, 15 Oct.
- the sun wages war with love and gives life to the entire universe, 9 Feb.
- resolve your problems by manifesting love and kindness, 24 May
- living exclusively on the love expressed by a look, 2 Apr.
- true intelligence that drives out fear, 7 June
- link yourself to the source of divine love, 2 Aug.
- protect it by living it in the subtle regions, 29 Aug.
- project your best feelings on the one you love, 10 Dec.
- renewing ourselves so that it endures, 14 Dec.

Love and wisdom – love is within us whereas wisdom is outside us, 19 Nov.

Divine **Love**
- raising ourselves up to this almighty magus, 13 Jan.
- its fire transforms our instincts, 24 June
- the only love that can fill your heart and soul, 15 Nov.

Pure **Love** is like a fountain of life, 28 Mar.

True **Love** – a subtle world that connects us with the whole universe, 27 Oct.

True **Love** makes you more beautiful, enlightens you and makes you happy, 15 Apr.

M

A **Magician** – how to become a black magician or a white magician, 9 Sept.

The **Master** advises his disciples according to their needs, 18 Nov.

Master, the – your divine self matters just as much to him as the celestial entities do, 13 Aug.

Matter
- with a materialistic philosophy, we end up crushed, 18 May
- on high, it is one with the spirit, 21 June

Meaning of life, the – we must look for it beyond the content, 2 Jan.

Meditation allows us to gather and store up spiritual energy, 7 Apr.

Meditation
- concentrate on light to link yourself with God, 4 June
- controlling our thought the same way we control a galloping horse, 10 July
- the mastication of an idea that provides a flow of energy, 7 Oct.

Metamorphosis (of the caterpillar) – a lesson from Cosmic Intelligence, 5 Aug.

Mistakes – correct them quickly, 19 May

Moderation – practising it so that the best things do not become harmful, 27 July

Moon, the – how to use the waxing or waning moon, 30 May

Moral Rules – the Initiates gave them to us to protect us, 20 Jan.

Morality – attuning ourselves with heaven, 16 Aug.

Music is not made to be understood, but to be felt, 22 June

N

Nationalism – only those who work for unity are right, 1 Mar.

Nature closes its doors to those who do not respect it, 23 Mar.

Nature – it will teach us if we know how to love and listen to it, 29 July

Lower **Nature** turns us into slaves, 20 Dec.

Lower and higher **Nature** – ignore the advice of your lower nature but follow that of your higher nature, 4 July

Negative Thoughts and Feelings – avoid them in order to be healthy, 24 Mar.

New currents – strengthening ourselves to withstand the tension they will produce, 21 Feb.

Nourishment obtained from the realms of the soul and the spirit is satisfying, 19 Dec.

Novelty – found by delving more deeply into the truths we thought we knew, 13 Mar.

Number 13 does not like impurities, and fights against them, the, 23 Nov.

Numbers – cosmic powers that organize all that exists in the universe, 17 Nov.

O

Old age brings clarity, wisdom, peace and joy, 3 Dec.

Opinions often stem from our basest needs, 15 Sept.

P

Past, present, future: study of the hands, face and skull, 16 Dec.

Paying – everything in life has to be paid for one way or another, 20 Oct.

Peace – to experience peace, work to harmonize everything, 8 Feb.

Perfection – do not be concerned about the time it takes to achieve it, 17 May

Philosophy – turn back to the philosophy of the Initiates, 27 Jan.

Philosophers' stone, the – a symbol of sublimation, of transformation, 16 Apr.

Philosophers' stone, the – more of a psychic process than a physical one, 26 Oct.

Physical plane, the – what you do below is reflected on the subtle planes, 6 May

Prayer
- find your happiness in the bond it creates between you and heaven, 12 Jan.

- going to the Source in order to seek luminous elements, 27 Nov.

Prayers, meditation and singing produce a light that can help humanity, 22 Mar.

Precautions – disciples must take them to protect themselves while they work, 31 Jan.

Preparation in the spiritual realm takes time, 29 Oct.

Pride in having accomplished our duty, 31 Dec.

Pride and vanity – influenced by Saturn and Jupiter, 4 Sept.

Primeval earth – it must become peaceful so that divinities may come and dwell within us, 5 May

Divine **Principle**, the – like a lamp always at our disposal, 25 Dec.

Problems
- if they are perpetually insoluble, change philosophies, 16 Mar.
- well-solved problems allow us to tackle the next ones, 22 Oct.

Prodigal Son, the – returning to the house of our heavenly Father, 10 Feb.

Progress – God has given us the means to make infinite progress, 19 Feb.

Purification is the work of a lifetime, 22 Apr.

Purity – important for our mental and physical health, 16 June

R

Divine **Realities** – we live the same ones despite our differences, 1 Oct.

True **Reality** is what we feel and experience, 17 Jan.

Recordings – our thoughts, feelings and actions are all recorded, 17 Aug.

Results – to obtain results, you must persevere in your spiritual work, 3 Jan.

Resurrection – once their cells have been awakened, human beings are no longer the same; their consciousness expands and they live in the dimension of the spirit, 4 Apr.

Revenge – leave it to the Lord, 6 Nov.

Royalty – disciples who are masters of themselves, 30 Dec.

S

Sacrifice – the transformation of all our impure elements into light and heat, 18 Apr.

Sagittarius symbolizes the triumph of reason over the forces of instinct, 21 Dec.

Seeds – if you plant them, all the powers of heaven and earth come into play, 29 Jan.

Self-control – learning to exercise one's willpower, 2 June

Sense of the sacred – by respecting the Divine, you respect human beings, 17 Apr.

Sensibility – it is developed when we reduce the quantity and increase the quality, 13 June

Sensitivity is proportional to evolution, 8 Mar.

Silence during our meditations lets us seek fusion with cosmic light, the, 24 Dec.

Silence is a quality of the inner life, 27 Aug.

Silence – the expression of perfection, 3 Apr.

Sing to awaken people's higher nature, 17 July

Situations – in the worst ones, we must think to remove ourselves or make amends, 29 Apr.

Society – changing it by first transforming ourselves, 18 Jan.

Soul, the – a physical body can be possessed but not the soul, 15 Mar.

Divine **Spark**, the – giving it favourable conditions to manifest itself, 12 Nov.

Spirit, the – matter is the form that contains and compresses it, 13 May

Spirit within you, the – it alone is capable of capturing divine energy, 24 Aug.

Divine **Spirit**, the – our only preoccupation must be to clear the way for it, 29 Dec.

Spirits of light – beautify your inner dwelling to benefit from their presence, 16 Jan.

Spirits of nature, the – invite them to work for the good of all humanity, 25 July

Spiritual bodies – we possess the three of them in seed form, 9 July

Spiritual exercises – finding the conditions of inner peace during the day, 31 May

Spiritual laws – apply them to achieve mastery of your psychic life, 23 Aug.

Spiritual life
- when disciples sincerely embrace it, the only thing that matters to them is their work in the world of light, 4 Jan.
- a soul cannot be prevented from going towards the light, 15 Aug.
- the harder the task, the more glorious the success, 14 Nov.

Spiritual love creates the right conditions for inspiration, 28 Dec.

Spiritual people – age is no disadvantage if they identify with the spirit, 19 Mar.

Spiritual qualities – focus your attention on them to make continual progress, 3 Mar.

Spiritual responsibilities – instead of crushing you, they lift you up, 19 Jan.

Spiritual riches – concentrate on them so as to accrue ever-lasting wealth, 5 Jan.

Spiritual sun, the – expose your seeds to its rays so that they may grow, 27 Mar.

Spiritual transformation happens in the blink of an eye following centuries of effort, 1 Jan.

Spiritual wealth attracts blessings, 28 Apr.

Spiritual work for the collectivity with abnegation, 13 Sept.

Spiritual work – strive to create a divine image of yourself, 26 Sept.

Stars, the – look and listen to them to feel at peace, 1 Aug.

Stars predispose but do not determine, the, 28 Aug.

Sun, the
- different entities inhabit its rays depending on their colour, 9 June
- nourishing our subtle bodies at sunrise, 13 July
- seek it out to learn about the laws of immortality, 14 Aug.
- capturing a spark that will bring you purity and light, 25 Aug.
- a symbol of the Lord: draw back the curtains to let Him in, 19 Oct.

The **Sun** is an example – it sends us messages but remains on high, 10 Mar.

T

Teaching, the
- methods to face the difficult conditions in life, 1 Sept.
- when properly applied, it harmonizes your whole life, 29 Nov.

Teaching of Christ, the – it was written for Westerners, 26 May

Temple, the – 'We are the temple of the living God.', 9 Mar.

True **Temple**, the
- a human being who has sanctified their spirit, 10 Jan.
- a hallowed human body, 3 July

Temptations – think about the consequences so as to resist them, 25 Oct.

Give **Thanks** until you feel that everything that happens to you is for your own good, 4 May

Thought
- living entities that can endure for a very long time, 13 Feb.
- its true power is on the causal plane, 26 Apr.
- subtle matter that can receive revelations from the universe, 15 June

Thoughts and feelings influence those who are prepared to pick up on them, 1 Feb.

Thoughts and feelings – take care to absorb ones that are pure, 22 Aug.

Divine **Thoughts** and desires bring us blessings, 7 July

Ties – forge them with beings who bring us closer to the Lord, 7 Aug.

Time – find time for the light or else your time will be spent in darkness, 19 Sept.

Transforming oneself
- do inner work and help will come, 22 July
- calling on the celestial fire so that it might melt us, and working by means of thought to create new forms, 31 July

Tree, the – how it corresponds to a human being, 15 May

Tree of Life, the – the angelic hierarchy between human beings and God, 6 Aug.

Trials
- heaven sends them to us so that we may improve ourselves, 8 Sept.
- start by accepting them and then loving them for the sake of your evolution, 2 Oct.

Trials of initiation take place in everyday life, the, 17 Sept.

Truth can only be grasped by the spirit, 30 Jan.

Truth – it is not always good to tell the truth, but it is always good to know it, 31 Aug.

U

Understanding is not separate from realization, 20 Aug.

Unity – inwardly we must learn to live the universal life, 18 July

Universal knowledge – obtained by living in harmony with the divine world, 5 Mar.

Universal Soul, the – uniting with it through prayer, contemplation and identification, 13 Oct.

Universal Soul, the – you can communicate with it at any time, 7 Jan.

V

Validate a philosophy before accepting it, 21 Apr.

Value – another virtue is making an appearance: brotherhood, 22 Nov.

Visiting friends –preparing to give them the most beautiful flowers and gifts by means of thought, 1 Apr.

W

Waste – lead a spiritual life to eliminate body waste, 23 Jan.

Water – flowing water has the power to remedy our negative states, 12 June

Water has the power to absorb both negative and positive elements, 21 Sept.

Water – physical water contains all the qualities of spiritual water, 3 June

White magic entails blessing objects, food and living beings, 21 Jan.

Winter symbolizes stagnation, the descent into selfishness, 2 Feb.

Wisdom – as it has appeared but recently in human beings, it is still fragile, 23 July

Word, the – the science of correspondences between letters and forces, 3 Feb.

Words
- watch what you say so as to improve the lives of those who are listening, 30 Aug.
- the power of speech can do miracles, 12 Dec.

Work
- think like an idealist and act like a materialist, 11 June
- the mind and the heart build together, 8 Nov.

The **Work** of a disciple – striving to make the spirit descend into matter, 24 Nov.

Divine **World**, the
- human beings must be conscious of its presence within them, 6 June
- gather riches there and distribute them to everyone, 22 Sept.
- gain access to it by harmonizing one's intellect, heart and will, 3 Oct.

The objective **World** and the subjective **World**
- recognizing the correspondences that exist between the two,
16 July
- scientists recognize that their science is limited to the five
senses, 20 July

Y

Young people – teach them the truths of initiatic science, 18 Dec.

Note: The three fundamental activities which characterize human beings are thinking (by means of the intellect or mind), feeling (by means of the heart), and doing (by means of the physical body). You must not believe that only the physical body is material; the heart and mind are also material instruments, but the matter of which they are made is far subtler than that of the physical body.

HIGHER NATURE

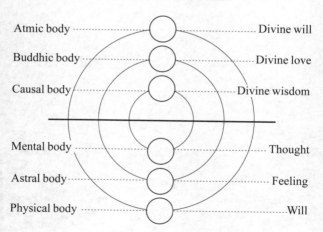

Atmic body	Divine will
Buddhic body	Divine love
Causal body	Divine wisdom
Mental body	Thought
Astral body	Feeling
Physical body	Will

LOWER NATURE

An age-old esoteric tradition teaches that the support or vehicle of feeling is the astral body, and that of the intellect, the mental body. But this trinity made up of our physical, astral, and mental bodies, constitutes our imperfect human nature, and the three faculties of thought, feeling, and action also exist on a higher level, their vehicles being respectively, the causal, buddhic, and atmic bodies which go to make up our divine self.

In the diagram, the three large concentric circles indicate the links which exist between the lower and the higher bodies. The physical body, which represents strength, will, and power on the material level, is linked to the atmic body, which represents divine power, strength, and will. The astral body, which represents our egotistical, personal feelings and desires, is linked to the buddhic body, which represents divine love. The mental body, which represents our ordinary, self-serving thoughts, is linked to the causal body, which represents divine wisdom.

*(Man's Psychic Life: Elements and Structures,
Izvor Collection No. 222, chap. 3)*

Introduction to the Sephirotic Tree

Jesus said, 'And this is eternal life, that they may know you, the only true God'.

For those who aspire to know the Creator of heaven and earth, to feel his presence, to enter into his infinity and his eternity, it is necessary to have a deep understanding of a system that explains the world. The system that seemed to me to be the best, the most extensive and at the same time the most precise I found in the cabbalistic tradition – the sephirotic Tree, the Tree of Life. Its knowledge offers the deepest, most structured, overall view of what we need to study and work on.

The cabbalists divide the universe into ten regions or ten sephiroth corresponding to the first ten numbers (the word 'sephirah' and its plural 'sephiroth' mean enumeration). Each sephirah is identified by means of five names: the name of God, the name of the sephirah, the name of the archangel at the head of the angelic order, the angelic order itself, and a planet. God directs these ten regions, but under a different name in each one. This is why the Cabbalah gives God ten names, each corresponding to different attributes. God is one, but manifests in a different way in each region.

This Tree of Life is presented as a very simple diagram, but its contents are inexhaustible. For me it is the key that allows the mysteries of creation to be deciphered. It is not meant to teach us astronomy or cosmology, and anyway no one can say exactly what the universe is or how it was created. This Tree represents an explanatory system of the world that is by nature mystical. Through meditation and contemplation and a life of saintliness, the exceptional minds that devised it came to grasp a cosmic reality, and it is essentially their teaching that survives to this day, passed down by tradition and continually taken up and meditated on through the centuries.

A spiritual Master is conscious of the responsibilities he is taking by allowing humans to enter this holy sanctuary, and so when you approach this knowledge you must do so with much humility, respect and reverence. By returning often to this diagram, you will find lights being switched on inside you. You will certainly never manage to explore all its riches, but from Malkuth to Kether this representation of an ideal world will always draw you higher.

TREE OF LIFE

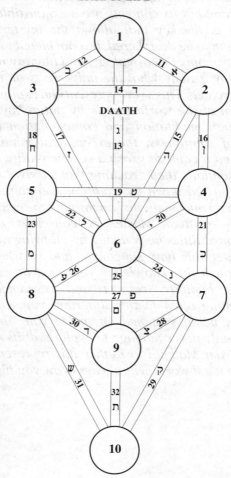

DAATH

TREE OF LIFE

1 Ehieh
Kether – *Crown*
Metatron
Hayoth haKadesch – *Seraphim*
Rashith haGalgalim – *First Swirlings (Neptune)*
♆

3 Jehovah	2 Yah
Binah – *Understanding*	Chokmah – *Wisdom*
Tzaphkiel	Raziel
Aralim – *Thrones*	Ophanim – *Cherubim*
Shabbathai – *Saturn*	Mazloth – *The Zodiac (Uranus)*
♄	♅

5 Elohim Gibor	4 El
Geburah – Severity	Chesed – *Mercy*
Kamaël	Tzsadkiel
Seraphim – Powers	Hashmalim – *Dominations*
Maadim – Mars	Tzedek– *Jupiter*
♂	♃

8 Elohim Tzebaoth	7 Jehovah Tzebaoth
Hod – *Glory*	Netzach – *Victory*
Raphaël	Haniel
Bnei-Elohim – *Archangels*	Elohim – *Principalities*
Kokab – *Mercury*	Noga – *Venus*
☿	♀

9 Shaddai El Hai	6 Eloha vaDaath
Yesod – *Foundation*	Tiphareth – *Beauty*
Gabriel	Mikhaël
Kerubim – *Angels*	Malakhim – *Virtues*
Levana – *Moon*	Shemesh – *Sun*
☽	☉

10 Adonai-Melek
Malkuth – *The Kingdom*
Uriel (Sandalfon)
Ishim – *Beatified Souls*
Olem Ha Yesodoth – *earth*
♁

Editor-Distributor
Editions Prosveta S.A. - F - 83600 Fréjus (France)
Tel. (33) 04 94 19 33 33 – Fax (33) 04 94 19 33 34
www.prosveta.fr – www.prosveta.com
international@prosveta.com
* Publisher in his own language - ** Distributor - *** POS

Distributors (*Updated list 12.08.2019*)

AUSTRALIA
  ** PROSVETA AUSTRALIA – Port Kennedy WA 6172
  Tel. (61) 8 9594 1145 – prosveta.au@aapt.net.au

CANADA
  ** PROSVETA Inc. – Canton-de-Hatley (Qc), J0B 2C0
  Tel. (819) 564-8212 – Fax. (819) 564-1823
  in Canada, call toll free: 1-800-854-8212
  prosveta@prosveta-canada.com – www.prosveta-canada.com

CYPRUS
  ** THE SOLAR CIVILISATION BOOKSHOP. – 1305 Nicosie
  Tél. 00357-22-377 503 – heavenlight@primehome.com - www.prosveta.com

GREAT BRITAIN – IRELAND
  ** PROSVETA – East Sussex TN 22 3JJ
  Tel. (44) (01825) 712988 – Fax (44) (01825) 713386
  orders@prosveta.co.uk – www.prosveta.co.uk

INDIA
  * VIJ BOOKS INDIA PVT. LTD. *(Anglais et Hindi)* – New Dehli - 110 002
  Tel. + 91-11-43596460, 011-65449971 – Fax +91-11-47340674
  vijbooks@rediffmail.com – www.vijbooks.com
  * BOOK MEDIA (Malayalam) – Kerala – www.indulekha.com/bookmedia
  Tél. +91 94 47 53 62 40 – bookmediaindia@gmail.com

ISRAEL
  * HADKEREN PUBLISHING HOUSE – P.O box 8426 – Tel-Aviv Jaffa 6108301
  www.hadkeren.co.il – talya@hadkeren.co.il

LEBANON
  ** PROSVETA LIBAN – P.O. Box 90-995 – Jdeidet-el-Metn, Beirut
  Tel. 961 (0) 3 448 560 – prosveta_lb@terra.net.lb – www.prosveta-liban.com

NEDERLAND
  * STICHTING PROSVETA NEDERLAND – 3871 TD Hoevelaken
  Tel. (31) 33 25 345 75 – Fax. (31) 33 25 803 20
  vermeulen@prosveta.nl – www.prosveta.nl

NORWAY
  * PROSVETA Norden – N-1502 Moss – info@prosveta.no – www.prosveta.no
  Tel. (47) 90 27 43 33 – Fax (47) 69 20 67 60

UNITED STATES
  ** PROSVETA Books – FBU USA - NY 11560 Locust Valley, New York
  Tel. (516) 674 4428 – prosvetausa@gmail.com – www.prosvetabooks.com
  ** WELLSPRINGS OF LIFE – Mount Shasta, CA 96067
  Tel (1) 530 918 3391 – wellspringsoflife@gmail.com – www.prosveta-usa.com

Printed in July 2020
by PRINTCORP

Dépôt légal : juillet 2020